Faith as Remembering

Faith as Remembering

Paul O. Ingram

CASCADE Books • Eugene, Oregon

FAITH AS REMEMBERING

Copyright © 2017 Paul O. Ingram. All rights reserved. Except for brief quotations in critical publications or reviews, no part of this book may be reproduced in any manner without prior written permission from the publisher. Write: Permissions, Wipf and Stock Publishers, 199 W. 8th Ave., Suite 3, Eugene, OR 97401.

Cascade Books
An Imprint of Wipf and Stock Publishers
199 W. 8th Ave., Suite 3
Eugene, OR 97401
www.wipfandstock.com

PAPERBACK ISBN: 978-1-5326-3099-6
HARDCOVER ISBN: 978-1-5326-3101-6
EBOOK ISBN: 978-1-5326-3100-9

Cataloging-in-Publication data:

Names: Ingram, Paul O., 1939–, author.

Title: Faith as remembering / Paul O. Ingram.

Description: vii + p. ; 23 cm—Includes bibliographical references and index.

Identifiers: ISBN: 978-1-5326-3099-6 (paperback) | ISBN: 978-1-5326-3101-6 (hardcover) | ISBN: 978-1-5326-3100-9 (ebook).

Subjects: LCSH: Religious pluralism | Christianity and other religions—Buddhism | Theology.

Classification: BR128 B8 I54 2017 (print) | BR128 (ebook).

Manufactured in the USA   OCTOBER 17, 2017

Contents

Preface | vii

1. Faith as Remembering | 1

2. God's Absolute Accessibility | 12

3. Just Who Is a Follower of the Historical Jesus? | 20

4. The Place of Honor: A Reflection on Luke 14:1, 7–14 | 27

5. Why Did It Take So Long? | 34

6. Is This All There Is? A Meditation on Philippians 2:5–9 | 39

7. A Beginner's Mind in a Mirror | 47

8. Why Should Christians Study the Buddhist Way (or Other Non-Christian Ways)? | 55

9. On Seeing, Scripture, and Tradition | 62

10. The Way of the Historical Jesus | 67

Contents

11. The Christ of Faith | 79

12. Unqualified Disciples | 87

13. Religious Pluralism | 93

14. A Meditation on Environmental Destruction | 113

15. The Pluralism of Life and Death | 118

Bibliography | 131
Index of Names | 135
Scripture Index | 138

Preface

One of my favorite writers is Eudora Welty. She once observed that the events of our lives occur in a sequence of time, but in their significance to ourselves they find their own order according to a time table not necessarily, perhaps not possibly, chronological. Time as we know it subjectively is often the chronologies that stories follow. Remembering our stories often seems like a continuous thread of revelation.[1] Process theologians like me would agree. In our memories of our past—our positive and negative prehensions—we make decisions that will affect our futures, which will in the next instant of time become conscious and unconscious memories upon which we construct new decisions that we take into our selves that in the next moment of time fade into memories that we will take in through a continuous process of self creation until we die. Hence, the title of this collection, *Faith as Remembering*.

Our memories of the past seldom happen in straight lines with chronological precision, but occur most often in spirals. The essays collected in this volume are all created out of my memories of past events that often, in unpredictable ways, pushed me to new insights about the nature of Christian faith that were often not desired, always unexpected, and always pushing me in new directions of theological reflection. But here's the rub: often, all too often, theologians write with an unintentional, and often intentional, Barthian-like universalism. This was not my goal in

1. Welty, *One's Writers Beginnings*, 75.

Preface

writing the essays in *Faith as Remembering*. These essays reflect my memories and are the source of the theological conclusions I have drawn as an historian of religions who now finds himself a practicing process theologian. As a process theologian, I can't even argue that the conclusions drawn in this collection of essays will be ones I can affirm in the future. All human knowledge is partial and incomplete and I may be in for new surprises as I continue practicing the art of theological reflection. I do not intend to universalize either my experiences of the past or my theological conclusions. But what I do hope is that the essays gathered together in *Faith as Remembering* will inspire readers to engage *their* memories as the foundation for drawing their own conclusions.

We live in an interdependent universe where things and events never exist in Cartesian isolation from the whole web of things and events ceaselessly undergoing interdependent processes of becoming. This includes the writing of books, as any honest writer knows by experience. No writer writes anything alone even when sitting in a study all hours of the day isolated from other human beings trying to figure out the perfect word or phrase. The people to whom we owe gratitude, living or dead, far outnumber the pages publishers generally allow for a preface. But at least I can take this opportunity to express my gratitude to the professionals at Cascade Books at Wipf and Stock for their support of my writing efforts over the years. In particular I am grateful to my editor, K. C. Hanson, for his encouragement of my work. K. C. is not only the editor in chief at Wipf & Stock, but an excellent biblical scholar whose work on the peasant culture of the historical Jesus, along with Douglas C. Oakman, have opened doors of New Testament scholarship that connect with my work as a historian of religions engaged in Christian theological reflection. This may sound like a bribe, but it's not: this book is dedicated to Dr. K. C. Hanson, teacher, critic, and friend.

Paul O. Ingram
Mukilteo, Washington

1

Faith as Remembering

Somewhere Stephen of Hungary (975–1038) once said, "Without a past, a nation has no future."[1] His words have a Whiteheadian ring about them. For the sake of our own futures, we must remember how the past has formed us in the present, what the past has brought us. This process involves positive and negative "prehensions" of the past, a process of bringing the past into the present as we anticipate future possibilities guided by our present individual "subjective aims" to achieve a wholeness greater than the sum of its parts. Of course, memories of the past are highly personal. According to Alfred North Whitehead, our *individual* subjective aims for ourselves are usually at odds with other individual's subjective aims for themselves and with God's initial aim that everything caught up in the field of space-time achieves an intensity of communal harmony in relation to all that exists and has existed in an interdependent harmony of wholeness and beauty greater than the sum of its parts. Process theologians refer to this as "the Commonwealth of God." But we only know what we have experienced, and we must remember what we know to have a

---

1. Stephen of Hungary lived between 975 and 1038 and is remembered for establishing Christianity as the state religion of Hungary.

meaningful, non-repetitive, future of creative possibilities, a future marked by what process theologians call "creative transformation."

It sounds quite easy, remembering what we know. But there is no better definition of faith. In remembering the past, we are drawn to future possibilities (God's initial aim for all things and events ceaselessly moving through space-time) that we must take into ourselves and somehow balance with our subjective aims for ourselves that are mostly in conflict with God's initial aim for us. Knowing and remembering are the *yin* and *yang* of faith, the defining polarities of faith.

Faith has little to do with "belief." "Beliefs" are opinions we assert without sufficient evidence to call our beliefs "knowledge." "I know something to be true or false" is different from "I believe something to be true or false." Beliefs may be true, false, stupid, irrelevant, superstitious, or just plain weird. Beliefs may even express faith. But beliefs do not engender faith. As Luther found out the hard way during a thunderstorm, no one has ever "believed" oneself into a state of faith. We *find* ourselves in a state of faith, of trust, and then must interpret the meaning of what we trust to understand what we are into, which is the function of theology, that is, "beliefs." Belief and doubt are two sides of the same coin whose only value is in an exchange of knowledge. They can crystallize as opinions that buy us nothing, or work for our profit as questions, for since both are really saying, "I don't know, but . . ." as they lead us back to ask, "What, then, is true?" And if questions are pursued in fact, not fancy, they will bring us to new knowledge. But only if we don't cling to the past we remember. It all begins with faith as remembering.

But if we are unfaithful, we forget. We forget our own experiences, which have shown us that the unknown exists and that we are contained in it. We know this because we always come up against the limits of our knowing and the fact that there is always something beyond what we know; because we have, if we are awake, experienced "miracles"—inner and outer events that cannot be explained by anything we "know."

It is certain that the unknown surrounds us. Mostly, we forget. But when we remember we know the unknown as much as it

Faith as Remembering

can be known, but never completely. Then we become open to it, feel ("prehend") our relationship with it, and understand by experience that it is the source of all knowing. Then we understand that it is the unknown that remembers us, and in remembering, we find ("prehend") our own meaning.

It took me a long time to grasp this. I graduated from Chapman College (now University) in 1961 with a split-major in philosophy and political science, both disciplines steeped in the Enlightenment mind-body dualism going back to Descartes; "objective" matters of observable "fact" placed in solitary confinement from "subjective" experiences of these "facts" as the sole method for discovering "truth" in all academic disciplines. The natural sciences became the model for this way of looking at things because of the huge successes in what the sciences reveal about natural processes, ranging from subatomic particles to biological processes in all living organisms to the cosmological structures of the universe itself. Even most of the courses I studied in seminary during my Claremont School of Theology days—courses in Biblical Studies, Theology, Church History, Pastoral Psychology, and my major interest, History of Religions—were all grounded in Enlightenment assumptions that assumed "truth" was something static and unchanging.

Nevertheless, I had questions. At a time in which Neo Orthodox theology was making absolute truth claims about Christian faith as superior to all other religious Ways, I remained deeply skeptical that any Religious Way could corner the market on truth about "the Sacred," as historians of religions often phrase it. I was then, and remain, a theological pluralist. I suppose this suspicion evolved as I encountered the sheer multiplicity of religious claims, some contradictory, some feeling like two sides of the same coin, some just plain stupid, some dangerous, some capable of harmonizing the religious pluralism ingredient in all religious Ways. So, the more I studied history of religions the less I felt it necessary to commit to any specific religious Way. I remained noncommittal regarding questions of normative truth, but deeply committed to describing the religious diversity of the Ways I studied, particularly in Japanese Buddhism, which was also the focus of my major professor, Floyd H. Ross.

Then in the fall semester of 1964, my last year in seminary, I bumped into John B. Cobb's seminar on Alfred North Whitehead. Cobb is one of the most skillful and patient teachers I ever experienced. He had to be, because reading Whitehead's major work, *Process and Reality*, is not easy for students trained in the presuppositions of substance philosophy and theology grounded in Descartes's mind-body dualisms. Whitehead's process view of reality is diametrically opposed to Enlightenment assumptions and paints an opposing metaphysical portrait. But reading *Process and Reality* for the first time was like trying to read a foreign language without prior knowledge of its grammar and vocabulary. So, like my father who was taught to swim when my grandfather threw him out of a boat into a cold Colorado lake, I jumped head first into process philosophy. And as I flailed around kicking and screaming for half the semester, Cobb finally threw me a rope.

I was very interested in symbolism and how symbols function in the world's religious Ways. During one of many visits to Cobb's office he suggested I might write a seminar paper comparing and contrasting Whitehead's understanding of symbolism with Paul Tillich's theory of how symbols function in theological reflection. As luck had it, I had written a paper on Tillich's understanding of symbols the previous semester for a seminar on Tillich's theology, so Cobb's suggestion seemed as good as anything I could come up with on my own. By the time I turned my paper in at the end of the semester, the scales had been lifted from my eyes as the elements of process philosophy began falling into place. While I wouldn't call this experience "revelatory," I found myself asking, "Why had it taken me so long?"

The first thing I discovered was just how useful the categories of process philosophy are for understanding one's own religious Way and the religious Ways other than one's own. Process philosophy, as opposed to Enlightenment philosophies, provides an amazingly useful hermeneutical ("interpretative") bridge by which to understand and interpret humanity's religious Ways without falsifying the experiences of persons actually practicing these Ways. The structuring parallels between the Buddhist's Way's worldview grounded in the universal experience of impermanence and Whitehead's understanding of process opened the Buddhist Way to me that has to this day been of great value in my work, particularly my work in Buddhist-Christian dialogue as well as interreligious dialogue in general. Later I discovered that process thought could make important contributions to science–religion dialogue. In fact, by the end of my seminar in Whitehead's philosophy I couldn't imagine anything that couldn't be clarified by the process categories of Whitehead's worldview. Things, or I should say "events," were brought together in a creative synthesis—from history of religions to the natural sciences to the processes of education to philosophy to economics—that to this day continue to amaze me. In short, I had discovered a worldview that literally pushed me into interreligious dialogue and interreligious dialogue with the natural sciences as a third partner. I had experienced an intellectual conversion.

Yet I sensed that something was missing. While I was immersed in the study of non-Christian religious Ways, my approach to Christian tradition was best characterized as "skeptical." I had taken numerous courses in theology and biblical studies from wonderful instructors during my seminary days. Still, I remained profoundly skeptical and resistant because of the sheer pluralism of two thousand years of Christian claims about the historical Jesus. I mean, just how many ways are there for understanding the history and meaning of the historical Jesus? Just how many views of the incarnation have evolved in the history of Christian teaching and practice? Which of these claims come closest to the truth of the actual events surrounding the historical Jesus? How many ways are there for confessing that the historical Jesus is the Christ of faith? And by the way, how and why did these confessions arise? Which of these confessions actually relate to life in the twentieth, and now the twenty-first, century?

These questions posed some hard issues. First, I discovered similar pluralisms ingredient in the non-Christian religious Ways I studied. Just how many portraits of the historical Buddha or Mohammed or Confucius are there? Which most accurately reflect these teacher's lives and teachings in their own historical contexts? Just how many ways are there of being a "Buddhist" or a "Muslim" or a "follower" of the Daoist or Confucian Ways? The pluralism I discovered in the Christian Way is reflected in all of humanity's religious Ways.

Second, if I was going to pursue research on interreligious dialogue I needed to immerse myself in the study of Christian historical and philosophical theology. And my world began to change in ways I never thought possible. An important part of this change was bumping into the work of Wilfred Cantwell Smith. As I read his book, *The Meaning and End of Religion*, more scales fell from my eyes.

According to Smith, there is no such thing as "religion." What he meant was that "religion" is a noun, a categorical abstraction that mostly Western scholars imposed on religious experience in the search for some defining "essence" by which to measure whether what religious people do is really "religious." He pointed out that there is no word for "religion" in the scriptures of the world's religious Ways and that "religion" is an "Enlightenment" invention, useful for missionaries trying to impose the Christian Way on Asian, Middle Eastern, African, South American, North American, Australian, and Pacific Islander cultures during the heyday of Euro-American colonialism, but having little relation to what "religious" persons believe and practice. In other words, human beings have been "religious" since shamans painted the shapes of animals in deep caves in Lascaux, France, and Altamira, Spain, 18,500 to 14,000 years ago without the abstractions inherent in the noun "religion" to define what they did and why they did it.

This meant, third, that the categories of process thought with its emphasis on internal relationships, subjective experience, interdependence, and process and becoming not only opened avenues by which I could explore non-Christian religious Ways, process thought also opened me up to the depths of Christian faith and practice. I was what Karl Rahner called an "anonymous Christian," meaning "a Christian without knowing it." To my utter amazement, I was in a process of theological conversion, an intellectual conversion with little experiential depth of the meaning of Christian faith. I studied the "words" of Christian faith, but I still didn't hear the "music" of Christian faith.

I don't mean that I had never worn the label "Christian." At age fifteen I joined up with a youth group called the "CYF" or "Christian Youth Fellowship" because I was chasing a girl. That didn't work out, but I eventually joined First Christian Church (Disciples of Christ) in Santa Monica, California. This required that I undergo baptism by immersion. I was previously baptized as an infant in the town of my birth, Pueblo, Colorado, at my father's United Brethren church. But the Disciples didn't recognize infant baptism or baptism by sprinkling. I had to have the full immersion. I am probably one of the few Lutherans who have been baptized twice. For Disciples, baptism was only offered to "adults" as a means of "washing one's sins away." But my friends tell me that even two baptisms were probably not enough.

The Disciples of Christ movement was the outgrowth of groups from various Protestant denominations (especially Presbyterian and Baptist) coming together in the nineteenth century, with early leaders Thomas and Alexander Campbell (father and son) and Barton Stone. More associated with the Anabaptist reaction against the Lutheran and Reformed traditions of American Protestantism, the Disciples claim to have no unifying theological doctrines or liturgy. Some local congregations are quite progressive, but most are fairly conservative while some border on Pentecostal fundamentalism. The congregation I joined was rather progressive in its social outreach while the minister was theologically conservative.

In 1957, the year I began my freshman year at Chapman College, I decided to "enter the ministry." This goal lasted until my senior year. By this time, "being a minister" just didn't fit into my developing interest in philosophy. The problem was that I had been accepted for admission to the School of Theology at Claremont, and I wasn't sure I should pursue this avenue of education given my decision not to pursue ministerial studies. I had to make a decision: either begin my studies at the School of Theology or get a job for which an undergraduate philosophy major was mostly useless, like the job I was offered selling soap for Procter & Gamble after graduation from Chapman.

But then my luck changed, or perhaps grace again was at work at this point of my life. New students at the School of Theology were required to visit the campus for an interview with a member of the faculty before the beginning of the academic year. The academic dean, F. Thomas Trotter, interviewed me. He listened patiently as I explained my decision not to become a Disciples of Christ minister and that I wasn't sure if seminary would be a good choice for me. When I finally stopped talking, he leaned back in his chair and flashed a grin. "Just give us a try," he said. "You may have decided the ministry isn't for you, but there are other avenues to pursue. You won't know which one until you try." So, I "gave it a try," and it was one of the best decisions I ever made.

The faculty at Claremont was incredibly excellent and diverse. Trotter taught a course in "Tragedy and the Christian View of Life." I had to plow through *Moby-Dick* in an undergraduate American literature course. But I had not made the connection between literature and theological reflection until under Trotter's direction I read it a second time. More scales fell from my eyes. The professors in Biblical Studies, Systematic and Philosophical Theology, Church History, and my eventual field, History of Religions were all great scholars and excellent teachers who helped me connect the life of the mind with the life of faith. I was beginning to connect theological lyrics with the music of Christian faith. I also disassociated myself from the Disciples of Christ.

Then in my second year at the School of Theology I met Regina Ruth Inslee. She graduated from the University of Redlands with a major in debate, speech, and sociology. Her father, Robert Ray Inslee, was according to the professionals in his field one of the most important church architects of his day. By the end of the academic year Gena and I were engaged and had set our marriage date for early August 1963. We moved into married student housing that September.

Faith as Remembering

My wife and her family were life-long Lutherans, first the Lutheran Church in America, which later merged with the American Lutheran Church to become the Evangelical Lutheran Church in America (ELCA) in the early 1980s. I didn't realize that the structure of Lutheran church services, at least in those days, followed the liturgical traditions of Roman Catholicism. There are differences, of course, that reflect Luther's break with Rome in the sixteenth century. Among other things, unlike Catholicism, confession is communal rather than individual. Lutherans do not often meet with their pastors to confess their sins and seek absolution. In Lutheran understanding, confession is communal and public and the pastor merely announces God's universal forgiveness to the whole community. The priesthood of all believers is a centerpiece of Lutheran theology, as is the notion that human beings can do nothing to earn "salvation" by anything human beings do or not do, that is, by "works." Like God's love, grace is an unearned gift that transforms human beings when they apprehend that they have been swimming in God's grace since birth while not knowing it. None of this, absolutely none, was taught, preached, or liturgically reenacted in the Disciples of Christ churches I had attended—which in fact ignored Christian liturgical tradition and theology.

While I was drinking all this in, Gena and I used to attended the dedications of church buildings designed by my father-in-law. It was a rather cheap date because Dad Inslee used to take everyone out to dinner to some very fancy Los Angeles restaurants. Before the services of dedication began, he would take Gena and me on a tour of the buildings and explain how he sculpted the theology of a specific denomination into the building's architecture. "Sculpting theology," "painting theology," literary theological reflection in poetry and novels and essays by writers like Ralph Waldo Emerson, Herman Melville, William Butler Yeats, Henry David Thoreau, Eudora Welty, Flannery O'Connor, Annie Dillard, Loren Eiseley, and other great literary figures was my final push into Christian faith.

But it was Lutheran liturgy that opened the door. I discovered that liturgy took me places I had never before imagined, often in the most unexpected ways. In the second century, persons seeking admission to the church did not receive catechetical instruction about the distinctive doctrines of the Christian Way. Instead they were gently led into the rhythms of liturgy—confession and forgiveness of sin, the repetition of creeds, singing hymns, listening to sermons, offering resources for the poor and needy, repeating the Lord's Prayer, the reception of the Eucharist. It wasn't until early Christian "newbies" had participated in the beauty and rhythms of liturgy for at least a year that they received catechetical instruction in Christian doctrines and creeds. This ancient pedagogical practice reflects my experience. Liturgy helped me hear the "music" supporting the theological "lyrics" of Christian teachings and practices. And there was no going back. I became a Lutheran in 1966 in Indianola, Iowa, where I had assumed my first teaching gig at Simpson College, named after an Abolitionist preacher named Matthew Simpson.

As I look back at these events, different possibilities opened and I had to make choices in light of these possibilities. Of course, I could have chosen not to choose, which is nevertheless still a choice. We are never free from making choices, but we *are* free to choose which path to follow reflective of the incredible variety of choices we bump into in the course of our lives. In Whiteheadian language, we positively and negatively "prehend" our past and make choices, which sets up new possibilities and the necessity for making new choices, a continuing process we undergo *ad nauseam* until we die.

The events of my past could have led to different choices, which means the course of my life up to now would have been different. In Whiteheadian language, I could have followed God's "initial" aim for me or my "subjective aim" apart from God's initial aim, which means following my subjective aims in isolation from perceiving that my life is interdependent with all sentient beings and with God. Had I not chosen to major in philosophy; had I chosen to accept a permanent job offer selling soap for Procter & Gamble instead of following Professor Trotter's advice to give the School of Theology a try; had I not chosen to study philosophical

Faith as Remembering

theology under John Cobb; had I not listened to my Hebrew teacher's advice to "follow my bliss" and enter the Claremont Graduate University to pursue a doctorate and become a university professor; had I not married Regina or engaged with the Lutheran understanding of grace through faith alone as this is worked through in liturgical practice, I would have literally been a different "Paul Ingram" than the person writing these paragraphs. Remembering the past and comprehending it is the heart of faith, whether one is a Lutheran Christian, a Buddhist, a Muslim, a Hindu, a follower of the Confucian or Daoist Ways or both, a follower of one of the numerous aboriginal traditions, or an atheistic humanist.

Accordingly, faith as remembering teaches me two lessons. First, our memories lead us through time—forward and back, seldom in a straight line, most often in spirals. Each of us is moving and changing in relationship to others and to the world, and if one is grasped by Christian faith or for that matter Jewish or Islamic faith, to God. As we discover what our memories of the past teach us, we remember; remembering, we discover; and most intently do we discover when our separate memories converge. It is at points of convergence that I have experienced creative transformation.

Second, as a Lutheran, it strikes me as a bit glib to suggest that "faith" is reducible to "commitment to doctrines." While I am convinced that it is of utmost importance to guide the practice of faith through theological reflection, faith must never be reduced to belief in doctrinal propositions. The moment we do, doctrines will hide the reality to which they point. "Faith" is not doctrinal ideology. While guiding the practice of faith through the filter of theological constructs is "faith seeking understanding," as Anselm of Canterbury (1033–1109) put it, theological propositions are no more than pointers. As my Buddhist friends have taught me, if we cling to a pointer, we only have the pointer and we miss the reality to which the pointer "points."

What follows in the remaining chapters are some "pointers" that I hope will be useful for readers of this book. But keep this in mind: don't cling to "pointers," either yours or mine.

2

God's Absolute Accessibility

In the beginning was the Word, and the Word was with God, And the Word was God. He was in the beginning with God. All things came into being through him, and without him not one thing came into being. What has come into being in him was life, and the life was the light of all people. The light shines in the darkness, and the darkness did not overcome it. (John 1:1–5)

Historians of religions are not usually invited to preach at Lutheran university chapel services. But for reasons that still mystify me as well as my colleagues in the Religion Department at Pacific Lutheran University, some years ago I was invited to preach. The text assigned to me was the Prologue to the Gospel of John. Which, as luck would have it, is one of my favorite New Testament texts.

But why me? Historians of religions are mostly focused on descriptive questions: what religious people have done and are now doing without concern about normative truth questions about what religious people have done or are now doing. Following Enlightenment assumptions going back to René Descartes, historians of religion are taught to describe "objectively" the "phenomena" of "religious experience." Normative truth questions, that is, whether or not what religious people have done or are now doing corresponds to reality or make valid moral claims are left to philosophers and theologians. Such balkanization of academic disciplines means scholars representing these disciplines do not engage in any sort of interdisciplinary dialogue about areas of human experience, a formalism now running amok in higher education even in liberal arts colleges and universities.

Accordingly, historians of religions try to help students understand religious history and experience other than their own apart from imposing positively or negatively their own religious perspectives on the traditions they study. History of religions is not missiology, which is a good thing because it helps students wrestle with their own faith, or lack of faith, more deeply and clearly. Theological imperialism is the historic sin committed by Christians since the fourth century. Anyone who knows me understands that I am the sworn enemy of theological and religious imperialism. Still, undergraduate students will not let a historian of religions run from *their* normative questions and we soon find that it is necessary to wear two methodological hats in our teaching methods to help students confront their own understandings of the meaning of faith seeking understanding in a religiously pluralistic world. Descriptive questions and normative questions are utterly interdependent and only an intellectual coward will run from this interdependency.

But why did the Campus Ministry staff ask me to preach in chapel on the Prologue to the Gospel of John? They had never asked me to lead a chapel service before because they were deeply suspicious of my Lutheran orthodoxy, perhaps rightly so. Perhaps their curiosity got the better of them. Judging from the number of students and faculty colleagues filling the pews at Trinity Lutheran Church my guess is they were curious as well. What follows is what they heard.

In *Teaching a Stone to Talk,* Annie Dillard describes how after Robert Edwin Peary reached the North Pole in 1909 he discovered he had nowhere else special to go.[1] So he invented an imaginary

---

1. Dillard, *Teaching a Stone to Talk,* 18–19.

geographical point on the Arctic Ocean called "the pole of relative inaccessibility"—that imaginary point on the Arctic Ocean farthest from land in any direction. There is also a pole of relative inaccessibility on the Antarctic continent—that imaginary point of land farthest from salt water in any direction.

I suspect it is my love of mysticism that lead me to appropriate the pole of relative inaccessibility as a metaphor that helps me think theologically about how human beings have experienced and reflected about the Sacred. For I have come to think of God as the pole of relative inaccessibility farthest from theological speculation in all directions. After all, one of the few things we know about the reality we name God is that God is relatively inaccessible. Every religious Way I know anything about seems to agree about this in their conceptions of the Sacred, however it is named. God is that point of spirit farthest from every accessible point in all directions, which means that God is the pole of most trouble—at least for theologians and historians of religions like me. God is also—I take this as given—the pole of great price.

This is why John's Prologue always challenges and amazes me, and why it now functions like a Zen Buddhist *koan* for me because it has become an object of meditation in a way similar to the function of *koans* in the meditative practice of Buddhist monks and nuns. In *koan*-like brevity, with little explanation, John's Prologue mixes Hebraic creation traditions with Greek philosophical traditions in a way that allows the writer to proclaim that the relatively inaccessible God has always been *relatively* accessible in creation from the first moment of what we now call "the Big Bang," and that—counting back from our time—God became *absolutely* accessible in historical space-time two thousand years ago incarnated in the life and death of a particular human being located in a particular culture within a particular religious tradition.

That's quite a claim. No other religious Way makes one quite like it: God is absolutely accessible—in nature and the rough and tumble of historical existence; not only "in the beginning," but here and now and in the future; not only "dwelling among us" incarnated in a single human being two thousand years ago, but also here and now and in the future—incarnated "in, with, and under" nature and human beings.

So, I sometimes wonder if Christians who hear John's Prologue read or who read it themselves are sufficiently aware of conditions. If what I think the writer of John is saying is an accurate interpretation, we should lash ourselves to our pews. Pastors should pass out life vests and crash helmets along with their bulletins. My colleagues teaching New Testament at Pacific Lutheran University should tell their students when they come to this part of John's Gospel, "Fasten your seatbelts," as Bette Davis once said in an old movie, "it's going to be a bumpy ride."

Permit me to illustrate just how bumpy the ride can be. I think I first began to understand the absolute accessibility of the relative inaccessible God in nature while hiking alone on the Olympic Peninsula in Washington State about twenty-five years ago.[2] I followed a game trail through opaque, self-concealing forest that broke onto a boulder and driftwood covered beach. It was an old trail, mostly taken over by deer on their way to a nearby creek that emptied onto the beach. Hemlock and red cedar loomed overhead from a floor matted with feathery moss, as if pulled up by invisible wires into the coastal fog.

I walked onto the beach into a setting sun that painted everything orange—waves breaking hard on rocks, forest crowding the beach, fog hanging on the trees like gray cotton wool, light rain dimpling the creek losing itself in the breakers. Sharp sounds popped across the rocks on my left, and I saw two elk—a bull and a cow—run as if on cue over a small grass covered dune and disappear.

My thoughts drifted away from the forest, the earth, the sea, the light, the elk, and focused inside myself. I suddenly became sharply conscious of my own breathing—a cool, fresh sensation of energy rushing from the life of the earth into my chest, and then warm, moist air brushing against my face soft as a kiss as I exhaled. And then I knew: every breath I take draws the life of

---

2. This experience on the Olympic Peninsula later became the foundation of chapter 3 of Ingram, *Wrestling with the Ox*.

Faith as Remembering

creation into myself. I breathe in soft, saturated exhalations of red cedar and salmon berry bush, fire weed and wood fern, osprey and black bear, martin and blacktail deer, salmon and raven. I breathe in the same particles of air that form songs in the territorial calls of thrushes and give voice to humpback whales, lift the wings of bald eagles, and buzz in the hum of insects. I breathe in the earth, pass it on, and share it in equal measure with billions of other living creatures. I drink from the creek and it becomes me; and like the elk and the gulls hovering in the westerly wind, I bring the earth inside myself as food.

The interdependency of nature—God's intention that all creatures live in harmonious, interdependent balance—is an expression of God's creative word from the very beginning. It is a reflection of the light of God's love for God's creation, always there, stalking all things like cougars on the hunt. For how empty and incomplete would creation be without the sights and sounds and smells that make life alive: blackbirds quibbling like druids; horses galloping on a soft track; crows sounding like they're choking on bark; elk bugling like the sound of distant war games; the metallic ping of night hawks; the kindergarten band of crickets; the electric whine of hungry female mosquitoes; the Morse code of redheaded woodpeckers. And how empty creation would be without the presence and sounds of us: the birth cries of new born babies, the sounds of human speech, the verbal and auditory pictures of literature and music, the imagination of the visual arts, the abstractions of the sciences, the play of children and skillful athletes in competition, the laugher of lovers and friends and colleagues.

Of course, there is pain and great suffering in God's created order. Nature's interdependent balance is maintained through predator-prey relationships—life must eat life to survive. This too is part of God's creation. Pain is often cruel, and cruelty is always a mystery and a waste of pain, even for God. Furthermore, God's gift of freedom allows us to misuse our own creativity in inventive and hideously destructive ways that inflict pain on nature and on our own species. Looked at realistically, human beings seem to be blots on God's creation, because somehow, we didn't work out the

God's Absolute Accessibility

way God intended. To understand this, all you need do is look in the mirror when you get up in the morning. The face that pins you there with its double stare reflects the eyes of the most efficient and remorseless predator to have evolved on this planet. God may have intended nature to be balanced, harmonious, and interdependent, but it's also rough in nature, whether in a rain forest or in a human made urban jungle, where pain and cruelty often mask God's absolute accessibility.

And yet there is something else. According to John's use of Hebraic creation traditions in Genesis 1–11, predator or not, God, the creator of the universe, has created us—all of us—in God's "own image" by no process of mass production. Each of us is a specially designed reproduction of God's image, which implies there is a special place in creation that only we can fill. We have unique responsibilities before God that cannot be delegated to any other creature. Moreover, we have the capability of understanding God and loving God, which is in principle unique. Apprehending this unique relationship is first the embarrassment—and then the joy—of every single individual's aspirations and movements toward personal communion with God and with other creatures. For God's creative word is not only addressed to the world and to creatures in the world "in general," but to human beings "in particular." It is a word that calls us to the struggle for justice and compassion in the human community. It is a call to balance the needs of the human community with the needs of nature. Some of us have heard this Word, some of us have occasionally paid attention to it, some of us have asked it to go away.

Once upon a time, a group of Hebrew pilgrims did just that. They heard God's word bellowing on Mt. Sinai in thunder and smoke and found it too loud: "All the people saw the thunder and the lightening, and the noise of the trumpet, and the mountain smoking," a text in Exodus records. It scared them witless, and they asked Moses to beg God, please, never to speak directly to them again: "Let not God speak to us, lest we die." And God, pitying their self-consciousness, agreed to become relatively inaccessible

Faith as Remembering

to them. "Go say to the people," God instructed Moses, "Get into your tents again."

It's very difficult to undo our damage and ask God to come back after we have asked God to go away. Still, these Hebrews had a point. As the psalmist wrote, "Who shall ascend the hill of the Lord? Or who shall stand in his holy place?" These are good questions. The answer is, there is no one but us. There is no one else to send, not a clean hand, not a pure heart on the face of the earth, but only us—human beings made in God's image comforting ourselves with the notion that we have come, like the Hebrews at Sinai, at an awkward time. But there is not one of us; there never has been a generation of men and women who have lived well for even one day.

Yet some of us have imagined well, with honesty and art, the details of such a well-lived life worthy to ascend to the hill of God, and have described such a life with such grace that we sometimes mistake their visions for history, their visions for description, and fancy that human life has evolved. You learn this by studying any history at all, especially the lives of visionaries and artists. You learn it from Emerson and Yeats and Eliot; you learn it from Picasso and Dalí; you learn it from leaders in the struggle against racism and oppression like Martin Luther King and Mahatma Gandhi; you learn it from the writer of John's Prologue: we do not, because we cannot, ascend "to the hill of the Lord" by our own self-justifications because there is no hill to ascend; there never has been a hill to ascend to encounter God's creative word. It's the opposite. God's eternally creative word comes to us: through creation and—get this—enfleshed in the historical Jesus of Nazareth 2000 years ago, and now—get this too—as the Holy Spirit, pouring over us and everything else in nature the way light floods out darkness.

We need to have faith in this Light that has always enfleshed God's creation. Faith is trust. It is never reducible to creeds, theological opinions, doctrines, beliefs *about* God or the relation between the historical Jesus and God. Specifically, Christian faith is trust—betting one's life—that *whatever* we can learn will lead more fully into the light of God's truth. Even when at the moment what we learn seems to take us into a dark midnight of the soul, faith as trust does not quit, does not give up, does not intellectually cut and run. In faith, one lets go of one's ideas, does not cling to them, even to one's ideas of God, in the confidence that in this way we will see the light of God's creativity gracefully spilling over creation like a waterfall; absolutely accessible; in, with, and under everything; closer to us than our own breath.

3

Just Who Is a Follower of the Historical Jesus?[1]

When I first read Dietrich Bonheoffer's *Cost of Discipleship* I had some difficulty understanding what he meant by "discipleship." The following passage from Mark's Gospel helped clear things up for me. I don't mean that I have developed a "doctrine of Christian discipleship" similar to what is often preached as a kind of Christian ideology in fundamentalist churches: follow a rigid doctrinally defined moral ideology to prove you're worthy as a Christian. As a Lutheran, this sort of "works righteousness" turns me off like a switch because it is quite the opposite of what St. Paul, Augustine, Luther, and Bonheoffer meant by "discipleship." But mostly, it was during a conversation in a Seattle bar during a "theology on tap" meeting of my local congregation that the meaning of discipleship first dawned on. It hit me like a ton of bricks.

The focus of our discussion was Mark 9:33–40, which I have split into two scenes for reasons that I hope will become obvious. First, Mark 9:33–37:

---

1. An earlier version of this essay was published in Ingram, *Wrestling with God*, 21–25.

Just Who Is a Follower of the Historical Jesus?

> And they came to Capernaum; and when he was in the house he asked them, "What were you discussing on the way?" But they were silent; for on the way they had discussed with one another who was the greatest. And he sat down and called the twelve; and he said to them, "If any one would be first, he must be last of all and servant of all." And he took a child, and put him in the midst of them; and taking him in his arms, he said to them, "Whoever receives one such child in my name receives me; and whoever receives me, receives not me, but him who sent me." (9:33–37)

Jesus' question to Peter, "Who do you say that I am?" is the heart of Christian self-understanding and must be answered differently in every age. We do not live in the first century or the Middle Ages or the nineteenth century. Clinging to past images of Jesus and his relation to God simply will not do in our contemporary age of global religious and cultural pluralism. Not surprising, since Christians have been practicing faith within globally pluralistic contexts for two thousand years.

We still haven't got it right, even though the answer to Jesus' question to Peter is right in front of us, as it was for the disciples, stalking us like wolves at entrails. According to Mark's gospel, the disciples didn't get it right even though they followed Jesus around Palestine for perhaps a year. Jesus tried to tell them, yet they didn't understand until after he was killed.

The scene is this. Jesus and the disciples have returned to his home in Capernaum after an extended journey. On the way to Caesarea Philippi Jesus had questioned the disciples about his identity. Now on the way back home, the disciples are arguing about their own self-images. When Jesus questions them they fall into silent embarrassment because they have been arguing about the preeminence of self—over who is the greatest. They are like fundamentalists inhabiting all religious Ways, trapped in the conventional categories of their religious systems. They, like Jesus, are practicing "Jews."[2] But unlike Jesus, they cling to their

---

2. I have placed quotation marks around the word "Jews" because "Judaism," or what I prefer describing as "the "Jewish Way" did not exist before

culture's conventional religious Ways so tightly they can't hear the music behind the lyrics of Jesus' teachings. Like legalists and fundamentalists of all stripes in all religious traditions, their path is one of fabricating verbal argumentation, of imaging a self—or a community of selves—exalted above others at the center of their conventional world. Their trip with Jesus has not awakened them. Instead, they saw Jesus as their ticket to glory, to selfhood exalted.

So once more Jesus instructs them about discipleship. His teaching method is consistently to subvert their conventional notions of discipleship as assuring a preeminence of position. "He who would be first must be last," he says. To make one's self last means negating the absolute nature of one's self, of one's *persona*. This is why receiving Jesus and the one who sent him in Mark and elsewhere in other Gospel texts is exemplified as the receiving of a child—of one who has not yet developed a strong self-image, of one who has no rank or particular importance. It is Jesus who approaches the disciples and the readers of Mark as a child, with no rank or importance whatsoever. It is God who sent Jesus, who approaches the disciples and us as a child, not as the romanticized image of sweet innocence, but the weakest of the weak.

Our first response as readers of this text is to disassociate ourselves from the egotistical disciples. In previous verses, Jesus had just been speaking about the inevitability of his suffering and dying. And the disciples' insensitivity to Jesus' fate, combined with their crass egoism, is not a stance a reader is likely to embrace. But by a rhetorical slight-of-hand, the Markan Jesus directly addresses the reader—meaning us—through a series of paradoxical "if" and "whoever" statements: "If anyone would be first, he must

---

the destruction of the Jerusalem temple by the Romans in 70 CE, after which religious authority switched from the temple priesthood to local rabbis, who forged the Israelite and Judahite traditions into a unified religious Way known today as "Judaism." The communal centers of emerging Judaism were local synagogues ("assemblies") under the leadership of rabbis ("teachers"). Part of the evolution of the Jewish Way involved separating itself from the early Jesus movement, which simultaneously broke from the Jewish Way into a distinctive Christian Way centered in local churches. This separation probably wasn't complete until the fourth century, when Emperor Constantine declared the Christian Way as the official religious Way of the Roman Empire.

Just Who Is a Follower of the Historical Jesus?

be last of all and servant of all"; Whoever receives one such child in my name receives me"; "Whoever receives me, receives not me but him who sent me." In other words, anyone who would practice the Jesus Way must reverse the pattern of imagined expectations and conventional understandings of religious teachings and practices and plunge headlong into the paradoxical world of Jesus' "doubling-back" discourse, and therein enter of the kingdom of nobodies that is the Kingdom of God.

The experience of paradox is the experience of being bracketed between seemingly incompatible but nevertheless coexisting pairs of opposites. Even Mark's language about God is paradoxical. Who is the "who" that sent Jesus? Why does Mark not explicitly identify God as Jesus' sender. The Markan Jesus simply says that to receive the weakest of the weak is to receive him and "him who sent me." In the same way, the voice of God speaks from the heavens at Jesus' baptism in chapter 1:1, and again from a cloud at Jesus' transfiguration. Yet Mark fails to mention just whose voice is speaking. And again, when the Markan Jesus addresses his Father in Gethsemane, no voice is heard at all. But the author of Mark names Jesus as the Son of God and our assumption that the voices Mark allows us to hear are from God is not mistaken. What *is* mistaken is that we know what this means. Not only is Jesus impossible to identify in clear definitions, God is too. What, then, could it mean to be great?

Now Mark 9:38–40:

> John said to him, "Teacher, we saw a man casting out demons in your name, and we forbade him, because he was not following us." But Jesus said, "Do not forbid him; for no one who does a mighty work in my name will be able soon after to speak evil of me. For he who is not against us is for us."

Now the disciple John changes the question by latching onto the name of Jesus to bring up the issue of just who can be said to belong to the Jesus Way. After all, throughout Mark's gospel, Jesus harshly criticizes various groups of people: Pharisees, scribes, temple priests, tax collectors, and Roman political authorities.

Faith as Remembering

Who could blame John for concluding that the disciples constitute a well-defined exclusive group over against outsiders? Indeed, defining a social identity was an important issue for the early church, as it still is today. But party spirit does not come from receiving Jesus and God as one would receive a child, but from a fearful mind that draws artificial boundaries around people as a religious prophylaxis to protect a community from coming into contact with whatever it regards as threatening—the very boundaries that the historical Jesus had been at pains to undermine.

Like St. Paul, Jesus did not recommend party identity, but opened up community to anyone who is not against him. There are no fixed criteria for membership in the Jesus community—beyond the requirement that one not be against it. There is no permanent pattern of Christian self-identity, no gold card of membership. Jesus' teaching in Mark is pluralist not exclusive: they apply to all who are not against Jesus, not only Christians, but also non-Christians: Buddhists who revere Jesus as an awakened person, that is, a Bodhisattva; Muslims who revere Jesus as one of the greatest prophets; Jews who see Jesus as a reformer calling people to a renewed practice of Torah.

Of course, these non-Christians do not accept Christian *ideas* about Jesus. Yet Jesus' teaching recorded here in Mark makes no such stipulation. To be *for* Jesus does not necessarily mean accepting ideas *about* Jesus. Ideas about Jesus—creeds, doctrines, and theological constructions in general—flow out of conventional wisdom and are tied to historical and cultural contexts and are empty of unchanging essences or once-and-for-all timeless meanings. Note that Mark himself gives no clear definitions because the author of Mark is the first Christian deconstructionist. His Jesus and the God who sent Jesus shy away from self-definition. The Messiah is not the glory figure of the disciples' conventional expectations, but one who experiences the sufferings and sorrows and joys of a lived life. The follower of Jesus is not one who belongs to the proper group. Anyone who is not against Jesus is a follower of Jesus—a very pluralistic group, indeed.

Just Who Is a Follower of the Historical Jesus?

What does Mark teach us about following the way of Jesus two thousand years after the disciples tried and failed? I think Mark teaches us negative and positive lessons.

Negatively, Mark's deconstruction of human pretensions about who is greatest, along with claims that any single group of followers of Jesus has an exclusive claim on truth about Jesus and the one who sent Jesus, tells us that Christian faith is not about ripping biblical texts out of context as a means of proving who's really Christian and who's not. Mark's portrayal of Jesus teaches us that no human being and no religious community is greater than another human being or religious community. Mark teaches us that God doesn't give a damn about "religion," but cares about people and the rest of creation. Mark teaches us that faith is not adherence to a set of doctrinal propositions about Jesus and the one who sent Jesus. Mark teaches us that Jesus and the one who sent him cannot be contained by ritual and theological systems. Mark teaches us that clinging to conventional practices and conventional understandings that seek to lock God within the safe boundaries of our cultural expectations while excluding those who do not see things our way is not faith but unfaith. Mark teaches us that we should never reduce faith to belief in a set of doctrinal propositions, that we should never confuse theological reflection, which St. Anselm defined as "faith seeking understanding," with ideology.

Positively, Mark teaches us that we find Jesus and the one who sent Jesus incarnated in the ordinary; in loving relationships between people; in the struggle against economic, political, gender, and racial injustice; in the struggle for ecological justice that frees nature—God's creation—from human exploitation. We meet Jesus and the one who sent Jesus wherever and whenever persons work for justice. Following the way of Jesus is not a matter of membership in a particular Christian group or wearing a particular Christian label like "Lutheran" or "Roman Catholic" or Presbyterian" or "Baptist." The Jesus community that Mark envisions includes anyone who is not against Jesus: the socially engaged Buddhist layman Sulak Sivaraksa, who has time and again placed his life in danger for his criticism of the Thai government's financial involvement in the drug trade and sex trade of his country; Dr. Cecil Murray, retired senior pastor of the First AME Church in Los Angeles, whose educational vision and social outreach to all poor and racially oppressed people has become a model for similar social programs throughout Southern California; Mahatma Gandhi, who followed the principle of non-violence in his struggle to free his people from British colonialism; Gandhi's Muslim friend, Badshah Khan, who interpreted the Qur'an's teaching of *jihad* or "struggle" as non-violent resistance against the injustices of British colonialism; Martin Luther King, who apprehended Jesus and the one who sent Jesus in his fight against American racism. All are followers of the Jesus Way, as are each of us, when we feed the poor; when we refuse to oppress people because of gender, ethnicity, or race; when we do not confuse membership in the Jesus community with membership in any particular form of the institutional church. We are followers of Jesus and the one who sent Jesus when we refuse to destroy nature through unbridled consumerism. The Markan Jesus teaches us that we find Jesus and the one who sent Jesus incarnated in the Kingdom of God that is the Kingdom of Nobodies.

4

The Place of Honor

A Reflection on Luke 14:1, 7–14

Entering dialogue with persons living faithfully in the depths of a religious tradition other than one's own often clarifies the faith and practices of one's own tradition. Because such persons have "heard" the "lyrics" and the "music" of their religious faith, the authenticity of what they say and do can help Christians hear more deeply the music and lyrics of Christian faith. They can even provide an entry into the meaning of a Gospel text. Such faithful non-Christians are what paleontologist Loren Eiseley called "hidden teachers." Bumping into non-Christian hidden teachers are forms of the grace that envelops everything in this universe, from subatomic particles to us.

As someone who uses his work in history of religions as the foundation for his theological reflections, I have encountered numerous non-Christian "hidden teachers." One particular encounter was with an elderly Zen Buddhist monk in Japan in the summer of 2001. I was one of a number of persons invited to give a lecture at a week-long conference on a Buddhist text called the *Lotus Sutra*, which is one of the most widely revered Buddhist text in East Asia.

Faith as Remembering

Whenever I attend professional conferences I often tire of the scholarly abstractions of academics trying to impress one another, so I played hooky for a day and explored the small town that was the venue of our meeting. In the foothills north of town I found a small Zen Buddhist temple and bumped into the abbot—literally—on his way to rake a dry garden. He must have been in his eighties, but he seemed to possess more energy and liveliness than any person I have ever met. We talked for a while as he raked the white sand in the dry garden into intricate patterns and explained what I already knew from research on Zen, but in a less abstract way—that Zen gardens are objects of meditation. Which was a bit odd, since raking gardens is usually a chore left to novice monks. Each word the abbot uttered seemed to harmonize with the rhythm of his raking movements, which were focused and exact. Raking a dry garden is also an exercise in meditation and I had never seen anyone so fully concentrated and aware of their surroundings.

When he had finished raking, he stopped talking and headed back to the small room where he lived in deliberate simplicity. Although he did not ask me to tag along, somehow I knew he had wordlessly invited me to his room for afternoon tea—a rather small, elegantly simple square room with no furniture other than three meditation cushions and a black lacquer writing table in the middle of the floor facing a small alcove called the *tokonoma* or "place of honor." Traditionally, a *tokonoma* is a place where guests are seated on cushions on a floor covered with rice straw *tatami* mats in traditional Japanese homes and Buddhist monasteries. A flower arrangement or a hanging scroll or both decorate the place of honor, and honored guests sit with their backs to the hanging scroll and the flower arrangement.

The abbot, whose name was Ueda Roshii, was supposedly in "retirement," although at that time he was training twenty novice monks. When we entered his quarters, he motioned me to sit in front of the *tokonoma*, which had a wonderful flower arrangement he had created that morning, and a seven-hundred-year-old hanging scroll with calligraphy that read "thundering silence." Thomas Merton, who was a Trappist monk, wrote much of "entering the

The Place of Honor

silence," and it seemed that was what the Abbot and I had done. As we sat listening to our breathing, a young novice monk, head shaven and bald as a pealed grape, entered carrying green tea. Then after about thirty minutes of wordless conversation, I heard a sliding door slide open outside Ueda Roshii's quarters and then a voice too loud for a Buddhist monastery.[1]

"My name is Tanaka," the voice announced with some authority. "Please give this to Ueda Roshii and tell him Tanaka is here to see him."

Ueda Roshii, pointed to his right ear—a signal that I should listen. Then the bald-headed monk entered, grinning like an emoji happy face, bowed and handed Ueda Roshii a business card called an *omeishi* and announced, "Tanaka-san is here to see you."

Ueda Roshii's eye's narrowed into an angry stare. He handed the *omeshi* to me and said, "Ingram sensei, *yonde kudasai*, which means "Professor Ingram, please read."

An *omeshi* is an important object in Japan and most Japanese people carry them and pass them out to people they've just met or when they show up for an appointment. The Chinese characters on an *omeshi* tell much about its owner, which is the card's purpose. Mr. Tanaka's *omeshi* was covered in black Chinese characters and Japanese script on both sides. The first thing I noticed was that Mr. Tanaka was mayor of Nagoya. The second thing I noticed was that he had listed in calligraphy all his college degrees, honorary degrees, ranks and titles, board memberships, and other labels on both sides of the card. Had there been any more calligraphy, the card would have looked like a small black lacquer chip.

During other visits to Zen temples I had learned the hard way when to keep my mouth shut. So, I handed the *omeshi* back to Ueada Roshii, who said to the monk, "Tell that worthless bag of bones I don't know who he is. If he doesn't leave the temple

---

1. What follows is Ueada Roshii's reenactment of a story that has floated around in Zen tradition for years. I knew this at the time, but apparently, Mr. Tanaka did not. So, I just sat back, listened, and watched. An old Zen parable reenacted before my eyes. I don't think this was planned for my "instruction," but I was sitting in a Zen temple so who knows.

immediately, I'll call the police and have his worthless body thrown in jail for trespassing."

The monk flashed an ear-to-ear grin, bowed, left the room, and shut the sliding rice paper door after him. A few seconds later I heard the monk say, "Ueada Roshii says you're a worthless bag of bones and he doesn't know who you are. If you do not leave the temple immediately, he'll call the police and have your worthless body thrown in jail for trespassing."

Then the card's owner said, "*dame da na*," which can mean anything from "Oh shit" to "I'm such an idiot," followed by "*wasuremashita*," which means "I forgot." "Please return my business card." Then another silence. "Please tell Ueada Roshii Tanaka asks to see him."

The monk reentered Ueda Roshii's room and handed him the business card, who handed it to me without looking at it. All the titles, honors, and degrees were crossed out with a ball point pen, and the only word left was "Tanaka."

I handed the card back to Ueada Roshii, who said very loudly, "Ah, my old friend Tanaka. Please show him in."

It turned out that Ueada Roshii and Tanaka had been friends for fifty years, ever since their student days at Harvard University, where Ueada Roshii received a Phd in philosophy and Mr. Tanaka received a masters degree in English literature. Even better, I got to spend two more hours with two very wise Buddhists and learned something about the Gospel of Luke's portrayal of Jesus, namely that the conventional wisdom that celebrates honor and social standing is not wisdom, but an illusion.

Jesus, who had been invited to a Sabbath dinner at the home of a wealthy Pharisee noticed how the guests coveted the place of honor at the table, which was the place at the right of the host, who sat at the head of the table, with everyone else arranged according to their social standing and relationship to the host. The closer one was seated to the place of honor, the more "honor" one possessed. But Jesus' observation inverted the usual expectation of the Pharisee and his guests. Jesus had a habit of doing that and it always got him into trouble with powerfully conventional people.

The Place of Honor

He simply pointed out that those who try to claim a place of honor always run the risk of being asked by the host to sit further away, while those who choose a less coveted place may be asked to sit *in* the place of honor.

This is not just a simple lesson in etiquette because Jesus further instructed the Pharisee: "When you give a dinner or banquet, do not invite your friends or your brothers or your kinsmen or rich neighbors, lest they also invite you and you be repaid." Clearly, these were the sorts of people the rich Pharisee had invited to his banquet. And the point of Jesus' lesson is obvious and similar to a saying in the Sermon on the Mount: "If you love only those who love you, what reward have you?" In other words, Jesus said to the rich Pharisee, when you give a feast, invite the poor, the maimed, the lame, the blind, and you will be blessed *because they cannot repay you.*

Or retranslated into more contemporary language, "When you give a party, invite the riffraff, the homeless, the beggars, the ugly, those who can't pull themselves out of poverty, those who seemingly refuse to better themselves, those we think are lazy and undeserving, and you will be blessed because they cannot repay you." Jesus is telling us to socialize and eat with the very people that social convention regards as a blight on our community—the alcoholics, the drug addicts, the homeless, the dispossessed, all those caught in economic circumstances beyond their control that force them into poverty and into life choices most of us find unethical at best and disgusting at worst. Jesus not only wanted us to socialize with such people, but to seat them in the place of honor without regard to *our* social standing, *our* role in society, *our* economic standing, *our* professional standing—all of which are illusions in the Commonwealth of God, which is in reality a Commonwealth of nobodies. Or as Luther put it, we're all saints because we're all sinners.

Of course, this sounds like nonsense to most people obsessed with the conventions of establishing themselves in separation from others in the quest for honor, either among themselves or with God. For the rich Pharisee, it took the form of a religious legalism that taught that only those who had followed all the rules that defined the righteous conduct of pious folk were promised a seat at the messianic banquet when the Messiah finally arrives to set things straight in God's creation. This banquet was in the future and would happen at a time determined by God. But one could earn a seat at this future table here-and-now by living by the "instructions" set forth in the Torah as guided by *halakah,* meaning the specific ritual, dietary, and moral regulations that proscribed the behavior of "good people" and separated "good people" from "bad people." Being wealthy, having social standing, acquiring honors and prestige in the present were regarded as signs that one's invitation to the future Messiah's banquet was assured. Those who do not match up with the demands of *halakah* are excluded from this future banquet, just as they are excluded by the conventional wisdom that governs the lives of the Pharisees of our own time.

Jesus thereby sharply and completely rejected the implication that legally pure and sinless Pharisees would alone be present at the great messianic banquet. On the contrary, he denied that any such folk will be present, but that the guests at that table will bear a striking resemblance to the original Israel, the refugee slaves from Egypt, who at Sinai ate bread and drank wine in God's presence at the foot of a mountain. Far from being an exclusive table of society's finest, those who eat bread and drink wine in the Commonwealth of God will be the dispossessed, the undeserving, the rabble, the riffraff, where all who are invited occupy a place of honor the moment they show up, or even if they don't show up. The invitation is free and without strings, without regard to honors achieved or imagined. In other words, it's all about grace.

The Pharisees of Jesus' time, just like the Pharisees of our time, thought of the Commonwealth of God as a future reality, a not-yet state of perfected existence in relation to God completely other than what we experience here-and-now, a perfected existence we must earn by our deeds in the here-and-now. Jesus didn't think this was the case at all. For him, the Commonwealth of God was both a future and present here-and-now reality. We experience the Commonwealth of God here-and-now whenever the hungry are fed, wherever the sick have access to adequate health care, wherever justice is upheld, wherever systemic forms of social, political, racial, gender, and environmental oppression are resisted. For God is on the side of the marginalized and the oppressed. We even experience the Commonwealth God here-and-now where we are, where all of us, right now, are sitting at the place of honor that is everyplace because we are so interdependent that the suffering of one of us is the suffering of all of us, just as the joy of one of us is the joy of all of us. We don't have to wait for the future because the future is already here. We don't have to wait for a future Messianic banquet, because we participate in this banquet every time we share the Eucharist. And there is no place of honor, other than the particular place we occupy at the moment we show up. So, let the party begin, an open invitation to all of us in spite of the religious labels we choose to wear or not wear, with no strings attached, and with utter disregard for all those conventional labels we use to define ourselves in separation from everyone else—an expression of God's grace that floods over the universe like a waterfall—or a tidal wave.

5

Why Did It Take So Long?

It was in 1976 when the meaning of Christian faith began to dawn on me, when, as St. Paul would have said, "it pleased the Lord to reveal his son to me." Not that I had a sudden flash of insight or heard voices or talked to Jesus as a kind of best buddy. My experience wasn't like being knocked off a horse, as it was for St. Paul. Nor did Christian faith catch me because of any specific thing I studied in seminary or did research on in graduate school. In fact, at the time, I wasn't even aware that anything had happened.

The occasion was a quiet conversation I had with one of my teachers under an escalator in a New Orleans hotel lobby during a national meeting of the American Academy of Religion. My theology professor at the Claremont School of Theology, John B. Cobb Jr., had just published a book entitled *Christ in a Pluralistic Age*. One chapter in this book called for dialogue between Christians and Buddhists. It was a wonderfully cutting edge piece of theological reflection, but I didn't agree with some of his interpretations of Buddhism. So, I wrote a critical review essay and sent it to him in advance of submitting it for publication in the *Journal of the American Academy of Religion* in order to give him a chance to tell me if I had misinterpreted or misunderstood his methodology or conclusions. Our first chance to talk was in New Orleans sitting on

Why Did It Take So Long?

the floor under an escalator in the main lobby of the conference hotel.

I was surprised and gratified that he liked what I had written—and the fact that I had written it—even though he thought some of my critique had missed several points he was trying to make. Our conversation was intense and serious, which is always John's way of dealing with people he trusts.

What I remember most about our conversation was my defensiveness about Christian tradition in general. Once in 1975, when I interviewed for my position at Pacific Lutheran University, the Chair of the Department of Religion asked me if I considered myself a Christian. I took a deep breath and said, "My problem with that question is that most people who publically identify themselves as Christians are so obnoxious about it." There was a great silence. "Especially now," I continued, "when the Christian right tries to ram their version of Christian faith down everyone's throats." I also said that I wondered if being a Christian was something we should claim for ourselves; I still agree with Kathleen Norris: if "being a Christian" means incarnating the love of Christ in my life, it would be best to let others tell me how well, or how badly, I'm doing.[1]

Besides, I wasn't sure I could wear the label "Christian" and still practice the craft of history of religions—an academic discipline that bills itself as a non-theological, non-normative, collection of descriptive methods for investigating religious traditions other than one's own. Anyone in my academic trade sees too much in the world's religious traditions that are creative and wonderful to make exclusivist claims about the superiority of one religious Way over another. I still cannot support religious imperialism of this sort. But historians of religions also see much in all religious traditions that seem self-destructive, irrational, exploitive, and irrelevant to contemporary life, and I wasn't sure I could be a Christian and an historian of religions simultaneously. Blinded by the Cartesian dualisms according to which I was trained in graduate

---

1. Norris, *The Cloister Walk*, 63–66.

school, I wasn't sure I *wanted* to wear any religious label because I thought it would hinder the "objectivity of my scholarship."

John had heard me say all this before—during my student days and in writing in some of my earlier publications, and in papers I had read at conferences about the proper methodology for studying religious "phenomena," meaning what religious people say, believe, and practice divorced from issues of the truth of what religious people say, believe, and practice. Finally, under an escalator in a New Orleans hotel he had enough of it and ended our conversation by gently saying, "You know, Paul, you're a Christian. Get over it. Christian faith is about trusting the truth in whatever dress it wears and following it no matter where it takes you."

The impact of these words didn't hit me right away, but looking back I think they initiated my journey into Christian faith. To this day, I wonder why it took so long. I find myself, shaped by a life in religious studies, the influence of Buddhism, a renewed commitment to life in Christ (understood Kathleen Norris style), and filled with a sense that somehow grace, however understood, flows more freely than anyone can imagine. So, in thinking back over the past forty years about how the journey of faith began for me, I thought I was going write this chapter about how the historical Jesus or St. Francis of Assisi began their journeys when they were in their thirties. But as I thought about this, it seemed pretentious. I'm sure there are plenty of biblical characters and Christian people who screwed up, devised a new heresy, or gave up the ghost in their thirties. So what? Instead, I decided to take some clues from the Twenty-third Psalm. Faith as a cup overflowing with grace is a much more compelling topic, and more to the point.

When Jews bless the cup of wine on the Sabbath, they often fill the cup and let it overflow, spilling a little on the table. This is to recall the psalmist's declaration that his cup is overflowing with the abundance and mercy of God. Knowing that my cup is always overflowing, no matter how it appears to my senses, has sustained me for over forty years.

One of the times I heard the Twenty-third Psalm publically read was 1999 at my father's funeral. The person who read the psalm read it badly, but still, it was the first time I really heard it. Why, I remember thinking, is this psalm so often read at funerals? Or during times of anxiety, fear, or danger? Psalm Twenty-three should be read every day.

This was the opinion of Rabbi Nachman of Bratzlaw. He said that all the Psalms should "be interpreted about oneself with regard to the war against the inclination towards evil, and its cohorts." Or in more Christian language, the Psalms in general and the Twenty-third Psalm in particular, are the prayers of Christ in us and the enemies are all internal. Thus, after studying the Hebrew meanings and the rabbinical commentaries, Psalm Twenty-Three has for me taken the form of a Christian *targum*, meaning a "paraphrased and expanded version" that captures what I believe is its meaning.

> The Lord is my shepherd, and by his grace, I never lack anything, no matter how it appears to my mind.
>
> He makes me to lie down in green pastures and leads me beside still waters—everything that sheep require, although my senses never see it that way.
>
> He restores my soul by causing me to repent,
>
> He leads me in the paths of righteousness for his name's sake, not because I deserve it or would ever walk the path even if I could find it.
>
> Though I walk through the valley of the shadow of death, I will fear no evil, for you are continually with me. Your rod and your staff comfort me, by keeping me from straying and by beating back the wolves in my mind that would devour me.
>
> You prepare a table before me—laden with everything I need—in the presence of my enemies, whose voices are tempting me to desire more than I have.
>
> You anoint my head with oil, thereby stilling those voices as I realize my true identity in Christ, the anointed one.
>
> My cup overflows with your poured out grace, freeing me to pour out myself for others.
>
> Surely goodness and mercy are pursuing me every day, and I will remain in the house of the Lord,

Faith as Remembering

the Commonwealth of God, and never leave that place which is beyond time and space.

The Twenty-third Psalm isn't a passive recitation or a mantra meant to help us get through a period of grief over someone's death. In the history of Christian spirituality, it is a method of practicing the "presence of Christ" by reminding us of what's real and what's not. Trusting this presence is called "faith."

Consequently, in the struggle against my mind and emotions, which are daily telling me things should be different, faith says, "It is finished." When my thoughts are filled with plans, schedules, projects, meetings, obligations, concern for the future, or worry about the next step in my academic agenda faith says, "Take no thought for tomorrow."

When I find myself manipulating people and circumstances to my advantage, or adjusting my words slightly to protect myself from scrutiny faith says, "Take no thought for your life."

When guilt leads me to try to change myself in a sincere effort to finally "get it right" or to gain more wisdom or understanding, faith says, "By one offering you have been perfected forever."

In other words, the Twenty-third Psalm is about "transcendence." Something is transcendent if it goes beyond ourselves, demands something of us, or lures us on to new levels of understanding and seeing that remind us that the universe is on God's shoulders, not ours. God is the shepherd, not us. The call of Christian faith—and faith as understood in non-Christian religious Ways—is to abandon our propensity to think that any moment should be different than it is.

We shall not lack. Our cup overflows. Right now. Forever. With no strings attached. And if we can trust the lessons of this Psalm we had better hang on and brace ourselves. Grace in the form of goodness and mercy should be overtaking us any minute now.

6

Is This All There Is?

A Meditation on Philippians 2:5–9

> *Let the same mind be in you that*
> *was in Christ Jesus, who though he*
> *was in the form of God, did not regard*
> *equality with God as something to be exploited,*
> *but emptied himself, taking the form of a slave,*
> *being born in human likeness, and being*
> *found in human form he humbled himself*
> *and became obedient to the point of death—*
> *even death on a cross.*

Contemplating the past and thinking about the future is one of those "universals of human experience" that has defined what it means to be human since Cro-Magnons painted the shapes of animals on the walls of deep caves in Lascaux, France, and Altamira, Spain, 18,500 to 14,000 years ago. Existence is a historical process for human beings and other sentient forms of life wherever life occurs, as well as for God. Process theology is particularly clear about this "fact": knowing where we came from helps us understand where we are now, which in turn gives us hints about how we might anticipate the future. For human beings, the construction of cosmologies—creation and origin myths that help us understand where we came from, where we are now, and where and how we might end up—are so pervasive across human history that one might be tempted to conclude that cosmological speculation is part of the human genetic code. In fact, I do not know of a single religious Way that does not structure its teachings, practices, and rituals according to some foundational cosmology. Cosmologies are one the ways cultures and persons wrestle with the Sacred named differently in all religious Ways.

The cosmological foundation of Judaism, Christianity, and Islam is a creation story. The Christian version of this story asserts that the universe originates in God's primal creative act, which God continues within the structures of the universe's natural processes until creation achieves God's intention, after which the universe as human beings now know it will end and be replaced by a "new creation."

According to current scientific opinion, the physical origin and end of the universe and its life processes center on Big Bang cosmology and evolutionary biology. The Big Bang and the theory of evolution are not "facts." But at this point in time, they offer the most convincing theoretical explanations of the evolution of the universe and its life forms and are the best scientific approximations we currently have. Both theories may be proven wrong. More likely both will be enfolded within a more comprehensive theory that will include a quantum theory of gravity.

Current scientific speculation about the origins of the universe and the origins of life coupled with an emerging consensus about the final end of the universe pose powerful challenges to all religious Ways, questions that often throw faithful men and women kicking and screaming into the reality therapy that Christians experience during the season of Lent. Here's how.

In 1988 two groups of astrophysicists, one led by Brian Schmidt and the other by Saul Perlmutter, using similar techniques were looking for a specific kind of explosion called a "Type 1a supernova," which occurs when an aging star destroys itself in

Is This All There Is?

a gigantic thermonuclear blast. Type 1a supernovas are so bright that their light can be seen all the way across the universe and is uniform enough to have its distance from the Earth calculated with a great degree of accuracy. This is important because, as Edwin Hubbell discovered, the whole universe is expanding in all directions at a given rate at any given time, which means that more distant galaxies are receding from the Earth faster than nearby galaxies. So Schmit's and Perlmutter's teams measured the distance to these supernovas (deduced from their brightness) and their speed of recession (deduced by the reddening of their light known as the Doppler shift).

When this information was finally gathered and analyzed, both teams knew something very quirky was going on. In the eighties, astrophysicists thought the universe's expansion would eventually slow down, either gradually or rapidly, depending on the amount of matter contained in the universe—an effect that was expected to show up as distant supernovas looking brighter than one would expect when compared to closer supernovas. But in fact, these distant supernovas were dimmer, which meant that the universe's expansion was speeding up, which in turn suggested that some sort of powerful "dark energy" now called antigravity is forcing the galaxies to fly apart even as gravity draws them together. Which means there is now more antigravity pushing the galaxies apart at an accelerating rate than there is gravity pulling the galaxies together. Which means the universe will continue expanding forever, unless forces now unknown to science are at work.

Given what cosmologists conclude about the universe's origins according to Big Bang theory and the fact that the universe will most probably infinitely expend, a picture of the universe's final end seems to be emerging in the scientific community. The hundred billion or so galaxies that can now be observed through the Hubbell telescope and telescopes on Earth will zip out of range. Tens of billions of years from now, the Milky Way will be the only galaxy detectable from Earth, although it's unlikely anything will be alive on our planet by then. Other nearby galaxies, including

Faith as Remembering

the Andromeda Galaxy, will have drifted into and merged with the Milky Way.

By this time, the sun will have shrunken to a white dwarf, giving little light and less heat to whatever is left on Earth as it enters into a long lingering death that could last a hundred trillion years—or a thousand times longer than the universe has existed to this date. The same will happen to most other stars, although a few will end as blazing supernovas. Finally, all that will be left of the universe will be black holes, the burnt our residue of stars, and whatever remains of dead planets.

Even this is not the end, according to Fred Adams, a University of Michigan astrophysicist, who has written much about the fate of the cosmos. Adams predicts that all matter at this stage of the universe's evolution will collapse into black holes. By the time the universe is one trillion trillion trillion trillion trillion trillion years old, these black holes will disintegrate into stray particles, which will bind loosely enough to form individual "atoms" the seize of today's universe. Eventually, even these will decay, leaving a featureless, infinitely large void. And that will be that—if this account of the universe's end is accurate or unless whatever inconceivable event that launched the original Big Bang should recur again.

The fact of the eventual futility of the universe over a time scale of trillion of years is not different than the theological problem this fact poses for the eventual futility of ourselves over a time scale of tens of years. If this is really all there is, the universe indeed seems pointless and empty of value and the metaphysical conclusions Steven Weinberg draws from Big Bang cosmology, Richard Dawkins's interpretation of evolutionary history, and E. O. Wilson's theories of social biology and genetic determinism appear as accurate descriptions of reality—the way things really are, as opposed to the way religious persons would like things to be. Christian, Jewish, and Islamic doctrines and practices—every one of them—are illusions having no basis in physical fact. So too Theravada and Mahayana Buddhist doctrines and practices, Hindu tradition, Confucian and Daoist traditions, as well as the

Is This All There Is?

primal traditions of native Americans and other aboriginal cultures, are likewise illusory. None of humanity's religious Ways can have any ontological correspondence to reality. Which means that all theologies of religion—exclusivist, inclusivist, or pluralistic—are meaningless. Which means that the practice of interreligious dialogue as a form of theological reflection is reflection on ideas without ontological correspondence to anything that can actually exist. If, of course this is all there is.

Still, we need to remind ourselves that scientific inquiry is very narrow and focused—bits and pieces of physical processes abstracted from their environing contexts and analyzed through repeatable experiments described mathematically. The intellectual power of the sciences comes at the price of ignoring what most human beings experience. For example, physics can inform us about why we hear sounds because of the vibrations on our eardrums at the impact of air molecules, but cannot explain my, or anyone else's, love of jazz or classical music or the poetry of William Butler Yeats.

But here the real hiccup: neither the Bible nor Christian faith and practice stake their claims on the foundations of scientific descriptions of physical fact, even though our faith and practices should be in dialogue with and informed by the natural sciences. Part of the experience of faith is the realization of universal impermanence, which is the heart of the Christian observance of Lent—the universe as cruciform. Lent reminds us that Planet Earth is not a paradise of hedonistic ease but a drama where life is learned and earned by labor, a drama where even pain and suffering drive us to make sense of things. Seen from the realism of Lent, life is advanced not only by thought and action, but by suffering and pathos, impermanent and transitory, governed impersonally by the Second Law of Thermodynamics. This is all there is, if your stop with Lent.

Christian experience apprehends that there is more than the truth of scientific descriptions of physical facts and that there is more than Lent. The pathetic element in existence for all living things about which Lent instructs us prepares us for the lesson of

Faith as Remembering

Easter: the pathos of God who empties God's self into the universe as suffering redeemer. The very metabolism of the whole universe needs to be understood as having both a Lenten and an Easter character. From this faith perspective, God met in physics as the divine wellspring from which matter-energy bubble up is in biology the suffering and resurrecting power that redeems life out of chaos. In other words, Lent and Easter teach us that the secret of life doesn't lie in molecules, natural selection, and the survival of the fittest. The secret of life is that it is a passion play. Things and events perish in tragedy. All religious Ways affirm this and evolutionary biology confirms it. Living things perish with a passing over in which the sacrificed individual flows into the river of life, a sacrifice to preserve a line, a blood sacrifice perishing that others may live. Trafficking directly with God, as the manna-eating wilderness generation did, or as the historical Jesus did, confers no immunity from death or suffering. You can live like a particle crashing and colliding about in a welter of materials with God, or you can live like a particle crashing and colliding about in a welter of materials without God. But you cannot live outside the welter of colliding particles.

Easter instructs us that the abundant life that Jesus talked about is a life of sacrificial suffering leading to something higher; that the spirit of God is a genius that makes life alive, that redeems life from death. Lent is not all there is. According to Philippians, God empties God's Self into the universe so that God takes up the finitude, suffering, and death of all existence in this space-time universe into God's Self. There is a divine "yes" deep within every "no" of nature's passion play. God rescues from suffering, but Christian faith never teaches that God eschews suffering. In the paradigm of the Cross, God empties God's Self by taking into God's Self the suffering and finitude of all things and events caught in the field of space-time. So, while Lent tells us that life is a passion play and that nature is cruciform, Easter tells us this isn't all there is.

I think something like this idea lies behind Saint Paul's portrayal Christ in Colossians 1:15–20:

Is This All There Is?

> He is the image of the invisible God, the first born of all creation; for in him all things were created, in heaven and on earth, visible and invisible . . . he is the beginning, the first born from the dead, that in everything he might be permanent. For in him all the fullness of God was pleased to dwell, and through him to reconcile to himself all things, whether in earth or in heaven.

In other words, the structure of Christian existence is kenotic: within the rough-and-tumble of impermanent space-time Lenten realities God empties God's Self into the universe. The structure of Christian experience bound up with hope in the universe's history is that of dying and rising. Each moment of space-time, as soon as it is realized perishes or "dies." A new moment truly lives only as it finds some novel possibility that is its own, appropriate to its unique situation, and worthy of realization in its own right. Living from our past is not a real option for Christians because if we seek life by clinging to past realizations, we do not live at all. Then it's only a question of the pace of death. The one who holds on to the past and repeats it does not enliven the past but only joins it in death. This is why conservatism and fundamentalism are theologies of death that never get past Lent. Easter teaches us that when we turn from the past in openness to the new we find the past restored and revitalized. It is when we think new thoughts and dream new dreams that our past thinking remains a vital contributing element, not when we endlessly repeat ourselves or try to defend what we thought in the past.

In other words, it is by dying that we live. And whatever redemption is, it encompasses more than humanity, past present, or future; redemption encompasses the whole natural order, every thing and event in the universe since the first instant of the Big Bang until the physical processes of this universe finally play out trillions of years into the future. For, as St. Paul put it, "God was in Christ reconciling the world to himself" (2 Corinthians 5:19). The deepest meaning of the universe, the meaning of 13.7 billion years of the universe's evolution from the Big Bang until now and the trillions of years to its final end—is that all of nature, every thing and event caught in the field of space time, is always united to God because God has taken all things into God's *kenosis,* God's *"self-emptying."* Nothing is left out that can be included. Absolutely nothing.

7

A Beginner's Mind in a Mirror

I've been thinking a lot about "God" lately. This is what theologians are supposed to do. But how can one think about a reality transcendent to all the distinctions, limitations and boundaries of thought and yet is immanent, deeply immanent, within all the distinctions, limitations, and boundaries of thought, apart from which there are no distinctions, limitations, and boundaries of thought? Paul Tillich never tired of declaring that God is "beyond" what theologians think and write when they write about God. "God" is "beyond God," he concluded. So, once more John Cobb did me no favors—or perhaps the best favor I have received from any teacher—when he declared in his living room some years ago, "Paul, you're a theologian." First, he said I was a Christian, and now I'm a theologian?

And of course, he left it to me to figure out what he meant—good teachers always do this to their students. I'm still trying to figure out what he meant. I mean here's my problem: to put it much too simply, historians of religions write "objectively" (àla Descartes) about religious matters of "fact"—what human beings have believed and practiced in different times and cultural contexts apart from concern about the "truth" of what religious human beings believe or practice. But theology is a "normative" discipline, or better, a collection of disciplines about issues of truth in all areas of human experience and concern, including what religious human beings have believed and practiced throughout human history rooted in experience (hopefully) of God, said to be simultaneously transcendent and immanent. But as an historian of religions, I am not "allowed" to make judgments about the truth, say, of a Christian or Buddhist teaching or practice I have described.

So now that I am a "theologian," the only thing I know is that I may have, as a Zen phrase puts it, "a beginner's mind." Maybe that's it! Doing theology requires a "beginner's mind," a mind kept fresh by what one does not know but wants disparately to know. And the more I think about it, the mystics seem close to the truth: "God" is hidden in a cloudy transcendence that continuously unfolds itself in the interdependent relational processes at play everywhere in the universe. We apprehend God in the dance of these ever-changing relationships: in the intimacy of lovers, in the love of parents and children, in the struggle for a just community, in our friends, in our interdependent relationships with nature, in sickness and health, for richer or poorer, in death that doesn't part us from relationship with God. Writing about this is the most difficult thing anyone can do. I certainly wouldn't have tried apart from John Cobb saying those magic words, "Paul, you're a theologian." So, I spent three days driving north on Interstate 5 from Claremont, California, to my home in Mukilteo, Washington, trying to figure out what the hell he meant. The result of this struggle was a book I wrote in 2012 titled *Theological Reflections at the Boundaries*.

Now, after reading Catherine Keller's *Cloud of the Impossible: Negative Theology and Planetary Entanglement*, I am further convinced that a "beginner's mind" is an absolute necessity for theological reflection. Keller was also one of Cobb's students, a process-feminist theologian who writes about apophatic mystical theology, meaning "negative theology of unsaying," as a process of entanglement in the Unknown, in a "cloud of unknowing." Read through the lenses of Whiteheadian process philosophy, the anonymous English author of the *Cloud of Unknowing* literally

A Beginner's Mind in a Mirror

"deconstructs" all affirmative kataphatic labels for God and all apophatic declarations of unsaying that deconstruct positive or "kataphatic" descriptions of God. The only thing left is that theological ideas, models, statements, symbols, icons—are metaphors that say more about human relationships and our relationships with nature than about "God." Which is not to say that theological metaphors are useless or do not sometimes disclose how we are entangled with each and every thing and event in the universe and with God—according to Whitehead's ontological principles as well as contemporary quantum physics—but never in the same way from moment to moment of space-time.

But, and here is Keller's point, not if we cling to our theological constructions. Metaphors—all metaphors—point to that which must sooner or later be "unsaid." A similar notion is found in the first chapter of the Daoist text, the *Dao de Ching*, or "Classic on the Way And Its Power": The Way that can be talked about is not the Way." Or again in Tilllich's words, "God is always beyond God," which I take to mean "the God that can be talked about is not God." All theological language is metaphorical. Metaphors are symbolic pointers. If one clings to a pointer, one has the pointer and over time what is pointed at recedes into a Cloud of Unknowing. Which is why theological reflection is a process that can never be completed. There are no finished theological systems, not even systems of fundamentalist certainties to which so many religious persons in all religious Ways so desperately cling. Accordingly, since Cobb now thinks I'm a theologian, I need to prehend (apprehend?) my own envelopment in the Cloud of Unknowing as I remember that my mind is always a "beginner's mind."

I think Marguerite Porete had such a beginner's mind when she wrote *The Mirror of Simple Souls*, for which she was burned at the stake for heresy on June 1, 1310, at the Place de la Grève in Paris. Marguerite was the only late medieval Christian mystic to be condemned and executed for heresy. I suspect one reason was that she was a woman who publically taught her mystical way to anyone who was interested. This was a dangerous thing to do in an age when public instruction in theology was reserved for celibate male clergy. Her mystical theology directly undermined the patriarchal authority of the Roman Catholic Church of her time, from papal authority to local clergy to the professors of theology at the University of Paris who condemned her for heresy.

She was from Hainaut in northern France and was a member of a group of religious women known as the Beguines, whose social status was somewhere between laity and clergy. Marguerite belonged to a distinguished line of thirteenth-century mystical writers that included Mechthild of Magdeburg and Hadewijch of Antwerp. Marguerite was associated with a movement called "the heresy of the free spirit" and her *Mirror* influenced the development of Meister Eckhart's mystical theology. Portions of Eckhart's sermons were condemned as heretical for reasons similar to those that led to Marguerite's condemnation. But unlike Marguerite, Eckhart was not arrested, tortured, or burned at the stake. The difference was one of gender.

Marguerite wrote the *Mirror* as a dramatic allegory in which five characters—Lady Love (Dame Amour), Annihilated Soul (L'Ame Anneantie), Reason (Raison), FarNear (Loingprès), and High Courtesy (Pure Courtoise)—engage in an extended discussion about the relation between love and theological reflection. In the process, the paradoxes of mystical union with God and the troubadour tradition of courtly love are brought into a beginner's mind in the language of mystical union with God.

To make a long text short, the high point of the drama occurs when Reason, who symbolizes the Aristotelian epistemology of the medieval scholastic schools and their theologians, is so perplexed by the mystical paradoxes of Lady Love that he dies. The dialogue that leads to Reason's death is a seven-tired cosmos of mystical stations, the fifth and sixth of which are the center of interest, while the seventh station is beyond all words and is associated by Lady love with the afterlife.

Early in the *Mirror*, Marguerite describes the "simple" soul as a soul whose will is annihilated by God's love. Such souls are (1) saved by faith apart from works, (2) exist only in love, (3) do nothing for God, (4) leave nothing for God to do, (5) can be taught

A Beginner's Mind in a Mirror

nothing, (6) from which nothing can be given or taken, and (7) have no will. Each of these traits of the liberated soul deliberately provokes Reason by directly criticizing the medieval Church's understanding of the way to salvation. The doctrines and practices of what Marguerite calls "Holy Church the Little" (the institutional and sacramental system of fourteenth-century Roman Catholicism) can be superseded only by the shock to Reason that Marguerite's description of the liberated soul in union with God entails. Reason, jolted to attention like a blind person whose sight is suddenly restored, demands an explanation from Lady Love.

Lady Love then describes a seven-stage process through which souls are led to union with God. These stages include the ascetic, churchly, and contemplative practices advocated by the majority of Christians of her day. In her description of the lower stages, Marguerite rejects the traditional forms of ascetic, ecstatic, and mystical piety particularly associated with women. According to her, the soul pass through seven stages, each initiated by God's grace, and marked by three "deaths": the death of sin, the death of nature, and the death of the spirit.

The Soul enters stage one after the initial death to sin, and is therefore given divine grace, freedom form mortal sin, and the ability to love God and the soul's neighbor. When this minimal Christian life seems inadequate, the soul is drawn into state 2. Here, the soul abandons all riches and honors in order to follow the evangelical counsel of perfection, of which the historical Jesus as the Christ of faith is the model. This initiates the soul's death to nature and leads to stage three. Now the soul possesses an abundance of love and desires to perform good works. Paradoxically, this leads the soul to give up all external works in order to be capable of greater love for God. Marguerite identified this state with the life of contemplation, ascetic piety, poverty, fasts, and prayer that is the center medieval monasticism.

Marguerite thought that most Christians of her day were stuck in the first three stages. These she described as "lost souls" stuck in "Holy Church the Little." Lost souls are incapable of attaining freedom because they refuse to see that asceticism, contemplation, and spiritual delight do not represent the soul's highest perfection Such practices—based on self-willed works—merely serve to absent the soul from God. But rather than understanding the divine absence to be a necessary part of union with God, lost souls who attempt to elicit experiences of divine joy through suffering, asceticism, and contemplative works are like "merchants" who think they can "barter" with God.

But some souls are drawn to stage four, where the first steps toward simplicity are experienced as having nothing to do with "works." This bewilders the soul because while still a "merchant" obsessed by will and works, souls at this stage recognize that bewilderment is better than nothing. This recognition leads to renunciation of will, which is stage five. Here, the soul recognizes its previous self-deceptions, which in turn generates fleeting experiences of the utter and complete transparency of the soul in union with God. This marks the death of the spirit, a two-fold death involving the death of reason and the death of will. This experience pushes the soul into stage six: union with God. Union with God is completed at stage seven, when the soul departs the body at death to be in eternal union with God.

According to Marguerite's mystical framework, when the soul experiences flashes of union with God at stage six, the soul shrinks into a smallness so great that it can no longer find itself because it has "fallen" into the certainty of knowing nothing and willing nothing. Now the soul is freed of desire, and will is disencumbered from all care for anything, including self, neighbors, or God. Having no desires and having abandoned all self-will, the soul reverts to a "pre-created state" of being, or in Marguerite's language, to "what the soul was when she was not." Liberated from its will (we would say "ego") the soul has no *why*, and acts "without a why" and "without a what." In other words, with "a beginner's mind." She writes:

> This is right, says Love, for her will is ours. She has crossed the Red Sea, her enemies have been drowned in it. Her pleasure is our will, through the purity of the unity of the will of the Deity where we have enclosed her.

A Beginner's Mind in a Mirror

> Her will is ours, for she has fallen from grace into perfection of the work of the Virtues, and from the virtues into Love, and from Love into Nothingness, and from Nothingness into clarification by God, who sees Himself with the eyes of His Majesty, who in this point has clarified her with Himself. And she is so dissolved in Him that she sees neither herself nor Him, and thus He sees completely Himself alone, by His divine goodness . . . Now he possesses [the will] without a why in the same way He possessed it before she was made a lady by it. There is no one except Him, and thus he alone loves completely, and sees Himself completely alone, and praises alone by His being Himself.[1]

In addition, Reason also dies because living without a why, with "a beginner's mind," means letting go of the distinctions and dualisms by which Reason (conventional scholastic philosophy and theology) function. Union with God entails complete abandonment of will, works, reasons, and self-vulnerability. Which means that union with God can occur only in the context of absolute trust, meaning faith. All defenses and desire for security are gone, and the soul in loving union with God no longer exists in the formal sense as a subject that wills and acts in relation to an object. The only will and action are the will and action of God, so that the annihilated soul is like a mirror free from the smudges of ego-centered self-effort because the annihilated souls is a self-reflection of God's will.

As a Lutheran, I might also add that Marguerite's *Mirror of Simple Souls* ends up with a "Luther-like" conclusion. Marguerite's mystical theology is a radical reconception of love, of God's love, and a vision of authentic Christian life not centered on acts or "works" that earn salvation, in her day meaning eternal life with God in Paradise. Any act done to achieve something from God that one thinks one does not already have is a "work" that engenders enslavement of the will: living according to conventional ethical virtues, participation in church sacraments, practicing monastic

---

1. Porete, *Mirror*, 167.

contemplative discipline. All these "works" are required activities for participation in "Holy Church the Little."

Although Marguerite's teaching about the soul—or as I as a process theologian would call "the self"—is not a conclusion that Luther would have supported, her understanding of "salvation by grace through faith alone" is pushed in her mystical Way to a conclusion that would have pleased Luther. The soul that gives up all will and works, who has a "beginner's mind" and "lives without a why" is no longer concerned with poverty or riches, honor or dishonor, heaven or hell, self and other, self and God. Such a state of utter selflessness only occurs when the soul is ravished by the grace of its divine lover. Or again in Marguerite's words "the One in whom she is does His work through her, for the sake of which she is entirely freed by the witness of God Himself . . . who is the worker of this work to the profit of this soul who no longer has within her any work."[2] In other words, because the liberated soul's own will or ego is annihilated by God's love, the soul lives a life reminiscent of what the Daoist sages called "actionless-action" (*wu-wei*) and Zen sages refer to as a "beginner's mind."

2. Ibid, 121.

8

Why Should Christians Study the Buddhist Way?

(Or Other Non-Christian Ways)?

I had my first encounter with the Buddhist Way in an undergraduate survey course in History of Religions at Chapman College (now University). The course's instructor was Ronald M. Huntington, an artist of a teacher who was also a master organist as well as a rigorous academic, who introduced his students to history of religions in a way I tried to emulate in my work with students. Whenever he lectured on the Hindu Way or the Buddhist Way students would swear he was a committed Hindu or Buddhist. The same experience happened when he lectured on Islam or the Jewish or Daoist or Confucian or Aboriginal Ways. It was Huntington whose introductions to the world's religious Ways aroused in me an interest in the Buddha and the Buddhist Way that continues to this day.

Of course, I can speak only for myself, but my academic study of both the Christian and Buddhist worldviews has been creatively transforming for several reasons. First, the Buddha's teaching about interdependence has helped me apprehend that Christian faith also rests squarely on the reality of interdependence. Nothing is separated from any other thing or event. We define who we are through webs of interdependent relationships: with family, friends, human beings we care about, both living and dead; with human beings we don't know or who injure us; with all life forms with whom we share Planet Earth; with every atom and subatomic particle in the universe because, as cosmologist Carl Sagan put it, "we are all star stuff." And for one who is a Lutheran, God is so incarnated within all things and events—past, present, and future—that no thing or event is ever separated from God or anyone or anything else in the universe, at least according to the Prologue to the Gospel of John. For God is incarnated in the interdependent relationships running amok in the universe at-all-times and in all places.

Second, the Buddha's teaching regarding non-self rings a truth that crosses religious boundaries. We are not permanent substantial "selves" or "souls that remain self-identical through time." We are a continuing series of interdependent relationships, none of which are permanent. Clinging to permanent selfhood in any form is the cause of the First Nobel Truth: all existence is suffering. Accordingly, we must learn not to cling to permanence in any way, shape, or form, which Buddhists are instructed to train themselves to accomplish by the "skillful means" of numerous forms of meditation. The Buddhist doctrine of non-self helped me apprehend that nowhere in the Tanak or the New Testament is there any notion that human beings possess a permanent substantial soul that survives the death of the physical body, a notion that originates in the substance metaphysics of Platonic and Aristotelian philosophy through which theologians from the third century on interpreted the New Testament.

Of course, I have only briefly noted what I understand is the value of my academic study of the Buddhist and Christian Ways. Nor have I exhausted my description of Buddhist influences on my theological reflections or the way I view life, all of which have originated in an intense academic encounter with the Buddha's Way that is still ongoing. But building on the preceding paragraphs, I

Why Should Christians Study the Buddhist Way?

will sketch my reasons for concluding that the academic study the Buddhist Way is of supreme importance for practicing Buddhists and Christians. But it must be kept in mind that I am *not* arguing that non-academic motivated followers of the Buddhist or Christian Ways are second-class Buddhists or Christians.

First, all the religious Ways that have engaged human commitment presuppose distinctive worldviews that are assumed by a religious Way's specific teachings and practices. The basics of the Buddhist Way are the doctrines of universal suffering, impermanence, and non-self ("the Three Marks of Existence") all of which the Buddha summarized by the Four Nobel Truths and which are interpreted through an amazing collection of Buddhist schools that have evolved over twenty-five hundred years. None of the traditions and schools of the Buddhist Way interpret the Buddha's originating worldview identically because they evolved in quite different cultural and historical contexts other than that in which the Buddha lived and taught. Here lies the source of the amazing pluralism inherent in the history of the Buddhist Way.

This situation is similar in Christian pluralistic teaching regarding the significance of the historical Jesus confessed to be the Christ of faith. Just how many Christological doctrines exist in Christian theological reflection and practice, the vast majority of which do not conform to the New Testament's depiction of the historical Jesus' religious practice and self-understanding? Similarly, how many versions of the historical Buddha and the Buddha of faith and practice are there? Which of these historically and socially constructed "Buddhas of faith and practice" most closely reflect the life and teachings of the historical Buddha?

Answering such questions requires that students of the Buddhist Way and Buddhist practitioners engage in a serious study of Buddhist history, teachings, and practices that focus on the historical development of the central teachings of the Buddha in his historical context twenty-five hundred years ago. Such academic study can be liberating because it frees followers of the Buddha's Way from clinging to any image of the historical Buddha or from absolutizing any particular Buddhist system of practice. Or in the words of a number of Zen teachers I have encountered, clinging to a socially constructed image of the Buddha is "killing the Buddha." The same is true when one clings to a particular practice or system of meditation. Which leads to my second point.

The central "skillful method" the Buddha instructed his monastic and lay followers to practice was the discipline of meditation. But the exact elements of the Buddha's own meditational practices are unclear, although he probably practiced some form of meditational Yoga. The point is that meditation is absolutely necessary for the attainment of Awakening—with the possible exception of Japanese Jōdō Shinshū (True Pure Land School). The sort of experience engendered by meditation is one in which the sense of duality—subject/object, good/bad, male/female, pleasure/pain, good/evil, self/other—disappears for a brief moment of time. Judging from how numerous Buddhist texts describe Awakening and how eminent Buddhist masters describe it, Awakening is an absolutely contentless experience that transcends the ability of language to capture. Such experiences are encountered in all the world's religious Ways, in Christian tradition generally referred to as "apophatic" or "unitive mystical experience."

But here's the hiccup. Anyone practicing meditation receives from that practice what a particular tradition trains one to expect to receive. That is, if persons actually achieve such a unitive experience, they interpret the meaning of this experience according to the doctrinal tradition that trains them. After all, Zen Buddhist nuns do not normally experience union with "Christ the Bridegroom." Nor do Benedictine nuns experience "Emptying" or *satori* through the practice of contemplative prayer. Religious human beings receive from a religious practice like Buddhist mediation or Christian contemplative prayer what the doctrines guiding their meditation train them to expect to experience. Interpretation is always part of what a person experiences through either Buddhist traditions of meditation or Christian traditions of contemplation. There is no such thing as an uninterpreted experience. So, if someone experiences a unitive experience like that apparently involved in the experience of Awakening, one understands the meaning

Why Should Christians Study the Buddhist Way?

of that experience in terms of what he or she expects before the experience occurs and as well what he or she expected after the experience has occurred. For me this fact makes it absolutely necessary to engage in serious academic study of Buddhist meditational traditions as well as Christian contemplative traditions. Buddhists living in the twenty-first century live and experience in different historical-cultural contexts than Buddhists in the sixth century BCE. The achievement of Awakening now is not identical with the Buddha's experience of Awaking twenty-five hundred years ago. My point is not that what Buddhist traditions preserve as the Buddha's meditative experiences and his interpretation of their meanings should not serve as a guide for contemporary Buddhists. My point is that tradition is only a guide, not something to cling to or absolutize in a manner similar to how Christian fundamentalists absolutize doctrines about the historical Jesus. Traditions are a guide for practice that must be applied to the different circumstances in which contemporary Buddhists find themselves. An academic study of the Buddhist Way or the Christian Way undercuts clinging to Buddhist or Christian traditions. Or as a distinguished Zen scholar, Masao Abe, once told me, we should not "stink of Buddhism or Christianity."

But an academic study of the Buddhist Way also enables one to see through ideas and practices posing as Buddhist, but which are not. As there is much religious snake oil posing as "Christian," so there exist forms of religious snake oil posing as "Buddhist." I hope the following account of an event that took place during an international conference on the Lotus Sutra in Japan in 2001 hosted by the lay Buddhist group Risshō Kōseikai (Society for the Establishment of Righteousness and Harmonious Interchange) will illustrate what I mean.[1]

The conference attendees were invited to a Sunday morning service at a local Risshō Kōsei Kai *kyōkai*, or "church." The

---

1. Risshō Kōsei Kai was founded in 1938 by Naganuma Myōkō (1889–1957) and Niwano Nikkyō (1906–1999) to spread Nichiren's teachings about the Lotus Sutra.

Faith as Remembering

congregation was seated in neat, straight rows on *tatami* mats separated by an aisle, while we as visitors sat in chairs in the rear. The service began when the minister, dressed in a black robe, entered as a group of young people processed down the aisle singing hymns praising the *Lotus Sutra*. (Many Japanese Buddhist lay groups picked up the Protestant flavor of this service from missionaries in the nineteenth century.)

Prior to his sermon, the minister invited a middle-aged woman to give her testimony. She tearfully recounted the conditions of her life prior to her conversion to the Buddhist Way because of the influence of Risshō Kōsei Kai missionaries in her neighborhood: her experiences of physical and emotional abuse by her husband, her long years of drug addiction, her rejection by her children and relatives, her life of poverty as a prostitute. But after she converted to Risshō Kōsei Kai, she said, her "negative karma was turned into positive karma": her husband no longer abused her, she recovered from drug addiction, her children and family now love her, and she no longer engaged in prostitution to make financial ends meet for her family. In other words, this woman blamed herself for her own abuse.

But then in a long sermon in Japanese, so did the minister. As I sat listening to his rather sharp condemnation of the woman before she became a member of Risshō Kōsei Kai, reconfirming her blame for her own abuse, I whispered to my friend, Mark Unno, "Am I hearing this correctly?"

Mark, who is a Pure Land Buddhist and an important scholar of Buddhist tradition, whispered, "Yes! Shut up!"

After the service ended, we were invited to meet the minister for tea and pastries. Mark went directly to the minister and dressed him down for using Buddhist teachings in such a patriarchal and sexist manner to condemn a very troubled woman whose husband and the other men in her life had so wrongly abused her. "She was not responsible for her abuse," he told the minister.

According to my worldview, while the testimony of this woman might have been a story of her experience of creative transformation, I also witnessed the power of creative transformation in

Why Should Christians Study the Buddhist Way?

the prophetic words and actions of a Buddhist scholar and friend. Christian tradition has too often been a source of oppression of women, blaming women for the abuse received from male clergy and laymen. Sadly, misogyny is rampant in all the world's religious Ways.

Finally, the most important reason for academically studying the twenty-five-hundred-year history of the Buddhist Way is that it leads, often in surprising ways, to experiences of creative transformation. There is immense satisfaction in intellectually comprehending the nuances, movements, philosophical debates, the origins of the various schools of Buddhist teaching and practice traditions, the interdependence between doctrinal teachings and what to look for in the practice of meditation, the connections between the Buddhist Way's evolution and its creative influences in the history and politics of the cultures in which the Buddhist Way has taken root—and the list goes on. In fact, there is immense intellectual satisfaction in the academic study of any religious tradition. The more one comprehends a religious Way's history the less parochial and self-centered one's own faith and practice becomes. This is true whether one is a Christian, Jew, Muslim, or Buddhist.

9

On Seeing, Scripture, and Tradition[1]

Once when the great god Śiva the Destroyer sported with his consort, Pārvati, she covered Śiva's eyes with her hands. Suddenly, the whole universe was plunged into darkness, for when Śiva's eyes are closed the universe is like a black hole with no light anywhere—except for the hidden fire of Śiva's third eye that always threatens the destruction of worlds. Hindu deities are said to be all-seeing and never close their eyes. From the near disaster of Śiva's and Pārvati's play, it's a good thing they do not. The well-being of the world is dependent on the open eyes of the gods. But the point of this Hindu tale is not about how Hindu gods "see" or how Hindus "see" God. The clue is this: it is not only the gods who must keep their eyes open; so must we in order to make contact with them and our deepest selves, and in the process, reap their blessings and secrets. Keeping our eyes open is called *darsán* ("seeing").

But here's the hiccup. Conscious experience of anything is very much a now-you-see-it-now-you-don't affair. A fish flashes in the creek that runs in front of my home when I lived in Tacoma, Washington, then before my eyes dissolves in water like salt. I

---

1. This chapter is a slight revision of material that originally appeared in Ingram, *Wrestling with the Ox*, 38–40; and Ingram, "On Seeing, Scripture, and Tradition."

On Seeing, Scripture, and Tradition

have seen elk and mountain lions ascend bodily into the heavens, and great blue herons and bald eagles fade into laves. Such events stunned me to silence. They say of experience that most of what exists nature conceals with stunning nonchalance, so that when we do see, vision seems like a deliberate gift, like the revelation of a dancer who for my eyes only flings away the seventh veil. Nature conceals as well as reveals.

This does not mean that seeing is merely sense data imprinting itself on a *tabula rasa* passive brain. Even at the level of physiology, seeing is an interpretative act—dare I say a "hermeneutical act." For human beings, seeing is largely a matter verbalization. Most of the time, we need words to call attention to what passes before our eyes, or we simply will not see it. We must have words for it, think and say them to describe what we are seeing as we see it, or chances are we will not see.

Of course, some things are hard not to see, and words seem beside the point: exploding volcanoes, storms, a beautiful spring day, a great blue heron gliding ghostly silent into a fog bank shrouding Puget Sound, or what Elijah is reported to have seen and heard while hiding for his life in a cave on Mount Horeb. But most of the time, if we want to notice anything, we must maintain a running verbal description of the present. Otherwise, we never know what's happening. This is ordinary seeing of which academic seeing is an example. When we see this way, we analyze, describe, theorize, sort, categorize, argue, debate, file, probe, and grapple with the world, often as seriously as Jacob wrestled with God at the River Jabbok. Then understanding what is seen becomes a function of questions asked, contexts embodied, methodologies followed, presuppositions consciously or unconsciously held.

But there is another kind of seeing, one that mystics in all Religious Ways regard as primary. This form of seeing is also an interpretation of what is seen, but it is different from ordinary seeing because it requires letting go of the instruments of seeing—our theories, assumptions, theologies, worldviews, our selves, and our purposes. Both ways of seeing are a bit like walking with and without a camera. When we walk with a camera, we walk from shot to

Faith as Remembering

shot reading the light as we go. When we walk without a camera, our own shutter opens as the moment's light imprints itself on our mind's shutter. When we see in this way, we are transfixed and emptied, and we become scrupulous observers.

To the person who sees this way, in what the Oglala Lakota shaman Black Elk described as "seeing in a sacred manner," it is less like seeing than being seen for the first time, as if knocked breathless by a powerful glance. It is the seeing of non-duality underlying diversity, apart from which there is no diversity, before unity is split into diversity by the verbalizations of the first kind of seeing. Mystics in all of humanity's religious Ways have seen in this "sacred manner." But they also interpreted the meaning of mystical seeing—before and after the experience of non-duality—verbally, according to the traditions that trained them to see. Mystical seeing and conventional seeing are interdependent, and theologians East and West have dedicated themselves to joining them together.

It's a lifetime struggle marking the literature of the world's spiritual geniuses. What this literature shows is that there are no hard and fast rules of interpretation. They discovered that the mind's muddy river carries along with it a ceaseless flow of ordinary trivial seeing, that it cannot be dammed, and trying to do so is a waste of effort that can lead to insanity. They discovered instead that we must allow the mind's muddy river to flow unchecked in the channels of consciousness so that once in a while we can raise our sights above trivia, look as we flow with it, mildly and with detachment, while gazing beyond it.

But our first hints of this nonverbal unity originate in conventional verbal seeing. The trick is learning not cling to the verbal clues—the error of fundamentalism in whatever religious Way it occurs—so that we can see over the channels bordering consciousness. Here, for those religious Ways that ground their teachings and practices in a scriptural tradition, scripture itself may point to a realm where words and events interact interdependently without utterance. Explaining this assertion requires reflection on the interrelation between scripture and tradition.

On Seeing, Scripture, and Tradition

Seen from the ordinary perspective of history of religions, "scripture" generically refers to an anthology of oral and written traditions that (1) express and transmit spoken and written words as sacred power, (2) engender meanings, values, ideals, cohesiveness, and communal identity defined through normative standards of behavior (3) relate a community to a reality experienced as sacred and transcendent, and (4) depict a path and exhort persons to follow it to establish interrelationships with this sacred reality.

Scripture fascinates because of its relation to tradition. It's a non-dual, heads-or-tails, chicken-and-egg affair in which scripture defines tradition as much as tradition defines the scripture that engendered it. Evidence abounds. Church tradition defined originally disparate pieces of Christian writing into a sacred canon that simultaneously created the evolution of Christian tradition and praxis—a process never officially ratified by any church council. Jewish tradition includes the oral traditions that Jews think underlie it. It is not limited to biblical writings and is constantly developing, so what Jews count as scripture defies categorization: it is neither exclusively legalistic nor narrative, neither history nor poetry. Certain sacred writings are recognized by all Jews. Others are sectarian and their authority is limited to a specific group, their sanctity possibly temporary. So, Jews do not so much "read" Torah and Talmud as "learn it." "Learning it" requires not only study of biblical texts but also detailed study of rabbinical commentaries whose content determines what scripture is.

Finally, Buddhist texts have been objects of intense veneration and study. Life and limb have been sacrificed to ensure their preservation and correct interpretation. Yet Buddhist tradition also asserts that its sacred texts have, in and of themselves, no inherent value. Their worth depends on what is done with them. In each of these Religious Ways, no scripture defines itself as "scripture" apart from "tradition" and no "tradition" exists apart from "scripture."

The universal interdependence of scripture and tradition has some startling implications, not the least of which is that scripture is capable of a diversity of interpretations, depending on questions asked. The answers discovered in turn become part of tradition.

There is, and always has been, more than one way to skin any scripture's meaning. This fact alone may make a collection of stories, legends, myths, legal injunctions, and narratives "scripture." All scriptures mirror the universals of human experience: life and death, joy and sorrow, creativity and tragedy, hope and fear, peace and violence, sacred and profane, all within a complex plurality of historical and cultural nuances. When tradition inflexibly dogmatizes a particular scripture as the true and only interpretation of the Sacred and our relation to it, that scripture's inherent flexibility vanishes along with its ability to function as "scripture." At worst the text becomes irrelevant to the ever-changing historical complexities of human existence, particularly in our present postmodern age of religious and secular pluralism. At best, dogmatized scripture becomes an object of mere academic curiosity.

But seeing the non-dual interrelation between scripture and tradition does not mean that all interpretations are equally truthful or valid or of equal worth. Faith and experience guided by intelligence and reason must guide hermeneutical praxis. Still, while all scriptures are capable of either exclusive or inclusive readings, there also exist more pluralistic possibilities generated by the questions inherent in postmodern experience of religious pluralism.

10

The Way of the Historical Jesus[1]

Both the Tanak and the New Testament preserve powerful communal memories of persons who experienced what are today called "apophatic" and "kataphatic" mystical experiences. One need only think of the prophets who spoke God's words to their specific communities, communities that always resisted the Torah's command that communities be grounded in justice—making sure that all persons have what is needed for meaningful existence, which may not be what persons desire—and compassion—a communal awareness that all human beings are so interdependent that the suffering of one is the suffering of all, and responding accordingly. Separate selfhood is a delusion, an egotistical deceit that separates human beings from God and the rest of nature. Or as Deutero-Isaiah phrased it, Israel is to be "a light to the nations," an example to be imitated within their own particular histories and cultural contexts. Of course, no such "light to the nations" has ever existed in human history. Nevertheless, the Jewish Way has for two-thousand years struggled against all odds to "repair the world" so that finally, communities centered on justice and

---

1. This chapter is based on a more fully developed discussion in Ingram, *Living without a Why*, ch. 7.

compassion might someday become the norm of human togetherness and human togetherness with God.

The Israelite tradition of Jesus' day preserved powerful communal memories of persons who experienced kataphatic and apophatic experiences. I have long thought that the historical Jesus was most certainly a Galilean shamanic mystic whose experiences motivated everything he did and said, particularly his political activism against the Roman power structure oppressing Judeans and Galileans. He experienced kataphatic visions, including a vision during his baptism, in which, as the prophet Ezekiel is recorded to have experienced, Jesus perceived "the heavens open" and the Spirit descending on him like a dove (Mark 1:10). Of particular importance was his journey alone into the desert as narrated in the temptation stories, but which historians of religions and anthropologists recognize as a wilderness ordeal or vision quest. In all probability, it was during his sojourn into the desert that Jesus experienced apophatic union with God. The exact methods of Jesus' contemplative practices are not known. But they were probably similar to the contemplative disciplines preserved in Judaism, Christianity, and Islamic mystical practices.

Other evidence that Jesus was a Galilean mystic can be seen in how he addressed God. His "God language" was very intimate, particularly his use of *Abba*, which is an Aramaic word that a small child would use to address his or her biological father. *Abba* is much like the English word "Dad," but Jesus also referred to God with female images and analogies. What such language expressed was the intimacy of his mystical awareness of God's presence everywhere at-all-times and in-all-places. The historical Jesus was not simply a person who *believed in* or had *an opinion about* the existence of God; he *knew* the existence of God *by experience*.

Evidence within the Synoptic Gospels and the general history of religions indicate that the historical Jesus was a particular type of religious person known cross-culturally. This evidence seems to undercut a pervasive notion in some evangelical and all fundamentalist expressions of the Christian Way that portray the historical Jesus a one-of-a-kind human being. Such notions of Jesus' uniqueness are linked to ideas that the Christian Way is the "only Way." Such religious imperialism has no relation to the historical Jesus, who claimed neither to be "God" nor the long awaited Messiah of Jewish expectations of his day and time. Rather than being the exclusive revelation of God, he was one of many mystical mediators of the Sacred in Israel's and Judah's history. My conclusion in this regard subtracts nothing from the importance of the historical Jesus for Christian faith and practice, but in fact adds to the credibility of both the historical Jesus *and* Christian faith. This is so because at the center of Jesus' life was a profound and continuous awareness of God's presence in, with, and under all things and events. What separated the historical Jesus from his contemporaries—and from most of us today—was that the life he lived and the death he died were wrapped up in his continual experience of God's presence.

Finally, like most mystics, the historical Jesus was a teacher of subversive wisdom—a "sage" as wisdom teachers are commonly called. There are two types of wisdom, which means there are two types of sages. "Conventional wisdom is the most common kind of wisdom and its teachers are "conventional sages." Conventional wisdom is what everybody knows because it represents a culture's understanding of what is real and how to live in accordance with what is real. The second type of wisdom is an alternative, subversive wisdom that undermines conventional wisdom while pointing to an alternative way of life. Its teachers are the subversive sages that populate the world's religious Ways. For example, the historical Buddha and the Daoist sage Zhuangzi taught Ways that lead away from conventional wisdom to "a road less traveled" whose basic character is "living without a why," as my favorite Christian mystic, Marguerite Porete described it. The same was true for the historical Jesus. His wisdom spoke of "the narrow way" that leads to life and subverts "the broad way" followed by conventional human beings, that leads to death.

It is well established that the historical Jesus was an oral teacher who like the Buddha and Confucius, relied on aphorisms and parables as his teaching method. Aphorisms are short easy-to-remember one-liners. Parables are essentially short stories. Together, the aphorisms and parables preserved in the Synoptic Gospels place readers directly in contact with the voice of the historical Jesus. One of the most certain things we know about Jesus, since he lived in an oral culture where literacy rates were quite low, was that he was a teller of stories and a speaker of great one-liners. Jesus' aphorisms and parables were invitational forms of speech. He used them to invite his hearers to apprehend something they might not have otherwise apprehended. In this way, Jesus' aphorisms and parables tease imagination into action, suggest more than they directly say, and invite a transformation of perception and understanding. In many ways, they function like koans in Zen Buddhist meditational practices.

Jesus' use of aphorisms, of which there are more than a hundred preserved in the Synoptic Gospels (Matthew, Mark, and Luke), are crystallizations of insights that invite further reflection, insights that more often than not stopped their hearers dead in their tracks:

> "You cannot serve two masters."
> "You cannot get grapes from a bramble bush."
> "If a blind person leads a blind person,
>   will they not both fall into a ditch?"
> "Leave the dead to bury the dead."
> "You strain out a gnat and swallow a camel."[2]

Jesus' aphorisms were in all probability spoken one at a time, but this is not how they are recorded in the Synoptic Gospels, where they are typically grouped into collections of sayings. Aphorisms are repeated many times, since no oral teacher, especially an itinerant teacher like Jesus, uses a one-liner only once. This means that their particular historical context described in the gospel narratives was not the sole context in which they were heard. It is

---

2. Luke 16:13 = Matt 6:24; Luke 6:44 = Matt 7:16; Luke 6:39 = Matt 5:13; Luke 9:60 = Matt 8:22; Matt 23:24. See, e.g., Hedrick, *The Wisdom of Jesus*, 103–17.

perhaps best to imagine Jesus' aphorisms as repeated bits of oral teaching employed many times on many occasions.

Some of Jesus' parables are very short, sometimes as brief as his aphorism, with the only difference being that parables are longer narratives. But Jesus' short parables, like aphorisms, are memorable, enigmatic sayings that are complete in themselves. For example:

> "To what should I compare the kingdom of God? It is like yeast that a woman took and mixed three measures of flower until all of it was leavened." (Luke 13:20 = Matt 13:33)

> "The kingdom of heaven is like a treasure hidden in field, which someone found and hid; then in his joy he goes and sells all that he has and buys that field." (Matt 23:44)

But most of Jesus' recorded parables are similar to short stories with plot and character development. It is probable that Jesus would have told them numerous times and may have expanded them to different lengths depending on his audience.

Jesus used aphorisms and parables to subvert the conventional wisdom of his day and replace it with subversive wisdom. "Conventional Wisdom" means the dominate wisdom of any culture, defined as that culture's taken-for-granted understanding of the way things are and the way we should live in accordance with the way things are. In other words, conventional wisdom summarizes a culture's dominate worldview. This means that conventional wisdom summarizes a culture's social construction of reality and the internalization of that construction within the collective psyches of individuals living in that culture. Thus, it covers everything from social etiquette to images of "the good life." Moreover, conventional wisdom is supported by systems of rewards and punishments. You reap what you sow; follow this way and all will go well; you receive what you deserve; the righteous will prosper. Politically, conventional wisdom is the ideological foundation of suppressive religious, social, political and economic domination systems of injustice.

Faith as Remembering

Like all mystical sages, the historical Jesus used subversive wisdom to shatter the conventional wisdom of his day. For example, what kind of world is it when a Samaritan—an outsider and ritually impure person—can be good, indeed the hero of a story told to Judeans? What kind of world is it when a Pharisee—conventionally viewed as righteous and pure—can be pronounced unrighteous and impure? What kind of world is it when riding bareback on a jackass is a symbol of kingship? What kind of world is it when purity is a matter of the heart and not a matter of external boundaries? In what kind of world are the humble exalted and the exalted humbled? What sort of world is it when the last will be first and the first last? The world Jesus described was the Commonwealth of God, which he compared to something small, like a mustard seed. He also likened the Commonwealth of God to something "impure," like a woman (whom his culture associated with impurity), and like putting leaven (which is impure) into flour. He also taught that the Commonwealth of God is for children, who in his world were nobodies, which means that the Commonwealth of God is a Commonwealth of nobodies. The Commonwealth of God is also for outcasts—for tax collectors, prostitutes, the poor, the sick, and the lame—and not for those whom conventional wisdom lifts up as worthy of God's favor.

So, like most sages, the historical Jesus spoke of two ways of life: a conventional way and a foolish way, a way of death and a way of life, a broad way and a narrow way. For example:

> "Enter through the narrow gate; for the gate is wide and the way is easy that leads to destruction, and there are many who take it. For the gate is narrow and the way is hard that leads to life, and there are few who find it." (Matt 7:13–14)

For most human beings everywhere, at all times, and in all places, the wise way is the conventionally easy way, while the foolish way is the path of disregard for conventional wisdom. Jesus reversed this understanding by teaching that the broad way of conventional wisdom is in reality, the way of foolishness that leads to personal and communal destruction. And like the prophets before him, he attacked the central values of his social world's culture: family, wealth, honor, purity, and conventional religion. It was against these values that he directed his most radical aphorisms and parables.

To cite one example, in Jesus' culture the family, which was a patriarchal structure, was the primary social unit and the center of personal identity and economic security. Thus a "good" family experiences God's blessings. But Jesus spoke of leaving family and hating family:

> "Whoever comes to me and does not hate father and mother, wife and children, brothers and sisters, yes and even life itself, cannot be my disciple." (Luke 14:26)

These words were probably directed against the patriarchal family structure, the primary social unit of Jesus' culture that was also a microcosm of the wider hierarchal social system in which he lived. The thing to note is that this aphorism is one of many instances of his use of the image of God as Father in a way that subverted the patriarchal assumptions of his culture.

Furthermore, Jesus understood fixation on the accumulation of wealth as idolatry:

> "You cannot serve God and wealth." (Matt 6:25/Luke 19:13)

He told numerous stories of people whose preoccupation with possessions caused them to miss the banquet to which everyone is invited. For example, one parable tells the story of a farmer who spent his life hording his goods into barns and suddenly died before he really began to live. Another parable describes a rich man who day-after-day ignored beggars at the gate (Matt 21:1–10 = Luke 14:16–24). Jesus ridiculed those concerned with honor, castigated those concerned with rules of purity, and indicted those who trusted their own religiosity.

His rejection of conventional wisdom is particularly evident in the way he experienced God. Jesus invited his hearers to apprehend God not as a judge who imposed punishment on those who did not follow "the rules," not as a deity whose requirements must be met, but as gracious and compassionately just. This is clear in two of his most familiar aphorisms:

> "Look at the birds of the air;
> > they neither sow nor reap nor gather into barns,
> > and yet your heavenly Father feeds them.
>
> Consider the lilies of the field, how they grow;
> > they neither toil nor spin
>
> yet I tell you,
> even Solomon in all his glory
> > was not clothed like one of these."
>
> (Matt 6:26-29 = Luke 12:24-27)

In other words, Jesus characterized reality—"the way things really" are as opposed to the way conventional wisdom asserts reality is—as overflowing with generosity and life. Yet there is also a deep realism in these sayings because in the very next line, Jesus spoke of the lilies of the field today being beautiful and tomorrow being thrown into ovens:

> "But if God so clothes the grass of the field,
> > which is alive today and tomorrow thrown into
> > > the oven,
>
> will he not much more clothe you—
> > you of little faith."
>
> (Matt 6:30 = Luke 12:28)

At the foundation of Jesus' teaching that God is the source of life who is both gracious and generous there is a deep reality therapy at work that recognizes the impermanence of life.

But for me, the parable that best summarizes Jesus' image of God as compassionately just is the parable of the Prodigal Son. New Testament scholar, Marcus Borg, set the drama of this parable into three acts.[3] In act one the Prodigal's Son's life is described in detail: a life of going into exile and becoming an outcast. He journeys to a far country, that is, a Gentile country and therefore an "impure land," where he not only squanders his money in "loose" living but, reduced to poverty, ends up as a fieldhand working for

---

3. Borg, *Meeting Jesus Again for the First Time*, 83–85.

a Gentile pig farmer. As a field hand working with pigs, he has become worse than untouchable, according to Israelite purity laws. Act 1 concludes with the Prodigal's coming to his senses and his decision to return home to his family.

The focus of act 2 is the father. Seeing his son approaching at a distance, he "has compassion" and rushes out to meet him. Brushing aside his son's prepared confession, the father with great joy clothes his son with his best robe, puts a ring on his finger, and sandals on his feet. Then he orders the preparation of a banquet in his son's honor.

Meanwhile, act 3 opens with the sounds of music and dancing floating over a distant field where the father's elder son is working. When the elder son finds out what's going on and why, he refuses to join the celebration and complains that he has been obedient and dutiful and was never so treated by his father. The father begs him to join the celebration, and the parable concludes with an unanswered question: will the elder son's conventional sense of the way things ought to be keep him away from the banquet?

I like this parable because of the way it subverts the conventional wisdom of Jesus' culture as well as our own. The elder son's voice is the voice of most human beings. But the real point, it seems to me, is that the parable of the prodigal son portrays a religious Way quite different than the way of conventional wisdom: a life of exile in a "far country" and a journey of return, but never to a life of duty, requirements, and rewards. In other words, the historical Jesus stood squarely within the Hebraic prophetic tradition. But living by subversive wisdom can be very dangerous. Or to paraphrase the way Dietrich Bonhoeffer put it, "When God calls you, God calls you to your death."[4] Not always a physical death, but always a death to conventional ways of living, according to which the majority of human beings, past and present, structure their lives.

Religious faith—according to all religious Ways—always places faithful persons at odds with conventional culture and the

---

4. Bonhoeffer's exact words were, "When Christ calls a man, he calls him to come and die." See Bonhoeffer, *The Cost of Discipleship*, 87.

domination systems of these cultures. This is so because faithful religious people find themselves unable to structure their lives according to the conventional worldviews of the majority of human beings. For this reason, "walking the way less traveled" can get a person killed, as Jesus experienced hanging on a cross.

But exactly what is the "narrow way" taught by the historical Jesus? According to Marcus Borg, the evidence indicates that Jesus invited his hearers to apprehend God as gracious and womb-like rather than as an enforcer of requirements and conventional legal boundaries. But more than this, Jesus' subversive wisdom was an invitation to a way of life leading away from conventional wisdom to life utterly centered in God. That is, Jesus' subversive wisdom understood faith as a deepening relationship with God. And finally, Jesus' subversive wisdom requires resistance against exploitative religious, social, political, and economic systems that oppress human beings in every culture in every period of human history. Standing squarely within the Hebraic prophetic traditions, compassion and justice are the foundation of human community and as such, are the *ying* and *yang* of God's call to human beings everywhere at all time and in all places.[5]

This aspect of Jesus' teachings brings up the question of the role of God's judgment. There are numerous teachings in the Synoptic Gospels where Jesus refers to a last judgment that has eternal consequences. But I am convinced that the notion that human life is primarily about measuring up to God's requirements so that human beings might earn a blessed afterlife was foreign to Jesus' teachings.[6] In all probability he did believe in the existence of an afterlife, but his specific teachings had little to do with how to get there. While some gospel passages portray Jesus speaking about a Last Judgment, being judged for one's sins was not central to his teachings about the narrow way.

---

5. See Ingram, *You Have Been Told What Is Good*, chs. 1–3. Also see Oakman, *The Political Aims of Jesus*, ch. 5; Oakman, *Jesus and the Peasants*; and Hanson and Oakman, *Palestine in the Time of Jesus*.

6. See Wright, *The Day the Revolution Began*.

Still, the notion of *historical* judgment was part of his teachings in much the same way as it was for the prophets who preceded him: blindness has its consequences for both individuals and societies. In both cases, living in the world of conventional wisdom is "living in the land of the dead." In our time, all one needs to do is read a newspaper or watch the nightly news on television to confirm the reality of historical judgment. We judge ourselves; this, not the threat of a hellish afterlife is that to which Jesus' teachings about judgment point. Furthermore, given the structure of existence inherent in Jesus' Way, it is highly unlikely that he referred to himself as Messiah or as God coming in the future to initiate the coming Commonwealth of God.

Jesus' narrow way is also portrayed by another image. He often spoke of the narrow way as the way of death: "Whoever does not carry the cross and follow me cannot be my disciple" (Luke 14:27 = Matt 10:38; Mark 8:34). Following the narrow way means dying to the world of conventional wisdom as the defining center of one's security. It also means dying to permanent selfhood. In other words, Jesus rejected clinging to permanent selfhood as the center of self-identity. Death is the ultimate letting go, the opposite of the clinging and grasping characteristic of the life of conventional wisdom. But the path of death for Jesus was simultaneously the path to new life. That is, it results in rebirth, a resurrection to life centered in God. Or restated in the language of process theology, the creative transformation of perception that the historical Jesus knew through his own mystical experiences is one to which he invited his hearers.

For these reasons, the Way of the historical Jesus represents a serious challenge to Christian tradition. This is so because following the Way of the historical Jesus entails moving away from conventional forms of Christian tradition to the subversive wisdom of the Jesus Way. Conventional Christianity is a way of being religious based on what one has heard from others. It consists in asserting that life is about believing stuff about what "the Bible says," or what the institutional church doctrinally teaches about what Christians are required to believe in order to be faithful. Either way, conventional Christianity reduces faith to belief in doctrines. But the Way of the historical Jesus points to a relationship to which the Bible and the theological traditions of the plurality of Christian thought and practices point: that reality Jesus experienced as God and the Spirit of God.

In other words, the historical Jesus' gospel is "the good news" of his own message—that there exists a way of living that moves beyond both secular and religious conventional wisdom. The creative transformation of which Jesus spoke leads from a life of requirements to a life of relationship with God and with everything that lives. The Way of Jesus replaces a life of anxiety with a life of peace and trust. It leads from the bondage of self-preoccupation to the freedom of self-forgetfulness. It leads from conventional life centered in cultural standards to a subversive way centered on God. It is, in other words, a way engendered by God's grace, as St. Paul, St. Augustine, the Church Fathers and Mothers, the mystics of Christian tradition, Thomas Aquinas, Martin Luther, and John Wesley, among others, knew and taught.

11

The Christ of Faith

As an historian of religions practicing the art of theological reflection who happens to be a Lutheran, I must confess that much Christian teaching about Jesus seems very confusing. I often feel intellectually and emotionally blindsided because I am not always clear about to whom Christians are referring when they talk about Jesus. This experience often happens when I listen to Sunday morning sermons. Accordingly, it is important to be absolutely clear about the terms employed in theological reflection about Jesus. Which "Jesus" are Christians and non-Christians talking about? And why?

For the sake of clarity in the preceding chapter and this chapter I need to clarify two important and interdependent notions. By "historical Jesus" I mean "Jesus" as reconstructed by historical scholarship. In this regard, my own predilections are mostly informed by the "Jesus Seminar," as well as the work of other historians, both Christians and non-Christians, trying to reconstruct the historical Jesus from canonical and non-canonical texts like the Gospel of Thomas.

Briefly stated, by "historical Jesus" I mean: a Galilean peasant born in or near the village of Nazareth between 6–4 BCE who around the age of thirty was baptized by John the Baptist. After his baptism and sojourn in the desert he spent approximately a year traveling in Galilee as an itinerant teacher leading a small band of disciples that included more than the twelve male disciples mentioned in the Synoptic Gospels. He spent the last week of his life teaching in and around the Jerusalem temple before Passover. As in Galilee, he found eager listeners, which angered both the temple priests and many (but not all) of the leaders of local synagogues because Jesus' popularity was construed by the occupying Romans as rebellion against their authority. During Passover, he was arrested by the temple leaders, charged with blasphemy, and handed over to the Roman military governor of Judah, Pontius Pilate, who executed Jesus by crucifixion around the year 30 CE.

Although he was baptized by John the Baptist, Jesus went beyond John's apocalyptic preaching about the immanent Reign of God. That is, when Jesus found his own voice, it was squarely within the Israelite and Judahite prophetic tradition's call for social, economic, and political justice that he connected with his own vision of the Reign, or better, Commonwealth of God. Unlike John the Baptist, Jesus taught that the Commonwealth of God was immediately present in the struggle for justice on behalf of the poor and marginalized. For him, justice and compassion were two sides of the same interdependent coin. God, whom he addressed as *Abba*, is directly experienced in compassionate and just relationships. Accordingly, for Jesus God's Commonwealth was decidedly for the poor. Finally, Jesus referred to himself neither as "Messiah" nor as "God."

I shall reserve the term "Jesus as the Christ" to mean "the Christ of faith" as portrayed in the four canonical gospels, particularly the epistles of St. Paul, the remaining texts of the New Testament, the creeds, Christian mystical theology, and theological reflection in general and Christian experience in particular. The Christ of faith is a theological interpretation of the historical Jesus. The historical Jesus and the Christ of faith are interdependent, but they are not identical and both are historical constructions. In the historical Jesus as the Christ of faith, Christians apprehend God active in history since the beginning of the universe, as exemplified by the prologue to the Gospel of John.

It is the Way of the historical Jesus, described in the previous chapter, that convinces me that he is also the Christ of Faith. By this I do not mean that the historical Jesus is God. I agree with the majority of New Testament scholars that Jesus did not think of himself as divine or even as the Messiah (in Greek, *Christos*), meaning someone appointed by God to free Israel from the oppression of foreign nations in order to establish a future world order to free Israel from oppressors with Jerusalem at the center. This means that the earliest witnesses to the historical Jesus—and his resurrection—were participants in Judean religious traditions, including St. Paul during his mystical experience of the risen Christ on the Damascus Road. They lived as a cognitive minority within the wider community of Judean and Galilean religious teachings and practices. Some of the disciples are reported to have experienced the resurrected Jesus (Matthew 28; on the road to Emmaus, in Luke 24:13–35, 36–49). Paul's and the disciple's experience of Jesus' presence after his death were most probably kataphatic experiences: visions, auditions, or simply sensing Jesus' presence. It was these experiences that convinced the disciples that the historical Jesus was the messiah who would usher in the Kingdom or Commonwealth of God, either in the near future or, as later New Testament writers concluded, at an undisclosed time of God's choosing. Furthermore, God's commonwealth would encompass all human beings and nature itself as "a new creation."

Of course, transforming the historical Jesus into the post-Easter Jesus declared to be the Messiah entailed for first-century followers of the Jesus Way a change in the meaning of "messiah," literally "anointed one," which originally referred to anointed kings of Israel and Judah. Furthermore, for two thousand years Christians have been debating and promoting creeds about the relationship between the historical Jesus and the Christ of faith. This is so because Christian faith and practice hangs on the experience that the pre-Easter Jesus (the historical Jesus) and the resurrected post-Easter Jesus was the Incarnation of God in historical space-time. Apart from early Christian experiences of the resurrection, the Christian Way would have probably reverted into Judean religion or perhaps simply vanished with the death of the earliest disciples—which was probably what the Romans who executed Jesus desired and hoped would happen.

As was the case in the early Jesus communities, so today no universally accepted understanding of either Jesus' resurrection or the Incarnation exists within the pluralism of contemporary scholarship or Christian communities. To be sure, most Christians assert *that* the resurrection occurred and that the historical Jesus is God's incarnation in history. But exactly what all this means remains a hot topic of discussion among theologians. I also suspect the majority of Christians sitting in pews along with most of their pastors are not particularly involved in this discussion, and do not care to be, even as they continue believing in the resurrection and the incarnation.

But for me, the categories of process theology best capture the early Jesus community's experiences of the historical Jesus as the Christ of faith. To genuinely hear the historical Jesus' subversive wisdom that radically, yet gently, points to his experience of God as compassionate and just means to experience Jesus as the Christ as an embodiment of the process of creative transformation at work everywhere in the universe at all times and in all places. Experiencing this subversive wisdom creates cognitive dissonance in relation to every existing theological, economic, social, and political system. It is when what the world takes for granted is rendered suspicious that one is open to the process of creative transformation modeled by the historical Jesus as the Christ of faith. Or as Reinhold Niebuhr more simply noted, Jesus afflicted the comfortable and comforted the afflicted.[1]

Of course, creative transformation occurs elsewhere through humanity's religious Ways. Sages—those mystics who experience the Sacred, however it is named or unnamed—transmitted subversive wisdom contextualized through the cultures underlying the religious Ways in which they lived and died. Sages like the Buddha,

1. Niebuhr, *The Nature and Destany of Man*, 2:35–51.

The Christ of Faith

Śankara, the Daoist mystics, Mohammed, the Sufi mystics, the Jewish sages, and other nameless sages too numerous to count incarnated and mediated the process of creative transformation to their communities. They still do. To think of the historical Jesus as God's incarnation does not require asserting that he was the first and only incarnation of the process of creative transformation that Christians think was at the heart of Jesus' experience of God.

But from the point of view of Christian faith and practice (which, again, *does not* invalidate or replace non-Christian religious Ways) in the historical Jesus as the Christ of faith human beings encounter God. Not everything that God is or is not, but nevertheless God. Consequently, the question for Christians is: exactly how was God related to the historical Jesus so that he became the Christ of Faith? Was Jesus only a shamanic mystic and teacher of subversive wisdom, or something else that emerged from his mystical experiences expressed through his subversive wisdom? Certainly, any attempt to describe the structure of existence of an individual is speculative inference, particularly when that individual lived two thousand years ago.

Yet for me, two characteristics of the sayings of the historical Jesus in his aphorisms and parables express: (1) an immediate and undistorted perception of the conditions of human existence, and (2) he spoke and acted with a peculiar authority that went far beyond the prophets of Israel and Judah, even as what he said and did was thoroughly grounded in this prophetic tradition. In other words, his structure of existence seems to have been grounded in his relationship with God.

Classical Christology asserts God's presence in the historical Jesus, but in a way that unintentionally denies his humanity. This reflects the substance metaphysics that underlies classical Greek philosophy through which early Christian memories of the historical Jesus were translated into the intellectual traditions of the Hellenistic world. Certainly, this process helped transform the original Jesus movement into a Way called "Christianity" separate from Israelite and Judahite traditions—particularly as first- and second-century theologians entered into heated debates about the relationship between God and the historical Jesus. Simply stated, Greek philosophy, undergirded by substance metaphysics, required that if the *logos*—God's word or creative action in the world—is present in Jesus, then some part of his human nature must have been displaced. Thus, as the Nicene Creed affirms, the defining substance or "stuff" that makes God "God," and the defining "stuff" that makes Jesus "human" existed in Jesus without "confusion." Hence, Jesus is both divine and human simultaneously, which is why he is declared to be "the Christ, the Son of the living God." In other words, in Jesus, two different substances or "stuffs" existed simultaneously—a notion that would have made Plato and Aristotle turn over in their graves.

Here's why. According to Greek substance metaphysics, every substance is different from every other substance. For example, all things and events are "formed substances," according to Aristotle. So, the substance "formed" into a human being and the substances formed into a dog or a cat or a tree or a deity are not identical. Therefore the question is, how can God's substance (the stuff formed into God and makes God "God" exist in a human being named Jesus (who was formed by a human substance) "without confusion." As far as I can tell, this puzzle has no coherent resolution if one sticks to the substance categories of Platonic and Aristotelian philosophy as a means of describing the historical Jesus' relation to God.

Accordingly, it seems to me that contemporary process philosophy provides the most coherent way of characterizing Jesus' relation to God. Process philosophy does so by abandoning the substance metaphysics of Greek philosophy while replacing it with a process category called "structure of existence." One way in which different structures of existence can be distinguished is by focusing on the constitution of the integrating center of experience, that is the "self" or the "I." When we were infants, this organizing center was controlled largely by our bodily experiences. Normal adult experiences, however, are constituted by memory of our past experiences. That is, adult experiences are largely organized in terms of purposes and memories inherited from the past. It is this historical route of experiences that constitutes our sense of who we are at any moment, that is, our self-identity through time during any present moment.

Yet all experiences of the divine presence are also incarnated in the form of God's "initial aim" at all moments of space-time since the beginning of space-time into what process thinkers, following Whitehead, refer to as "actual occasions of experience." God's initial aim is what is best for a particular actual occasion of experience at every moment of its existence in interdependence with every other actual occasion of experience in the universe. There is, however, tension between God's initial aim for an occasion and that occasion's "subjective aim" for itself. Accordingly, for the majority of human beings, the divine presence is experienced as other, even though it is "incarnated" in human beings as God's initial aim and is usually in tension with an occasion's subjective aim for itself. That is, most human beings experience God's presence as other, occasionally as gracious, often as judgmental, or simply absent.

But the evidence from Jesus' aphorisms and parables suggests that his structure of existence did not reflect this tension. This seems to be the case because from his baptism and subsequent journey into the Judean desert until his crucifixion, the historical Jesus' selfhood was constituted by God's agency as an initial aim in union with Jesus' own subjective aim for himself. According to Whitehead, God's initial aim for all occasions of experience—every thing and event in the universe at every moment of space-time—is that each occasion achieves the maximum self-fulfillment of which it is capable in interrelationship with the totality of occasions that constitute the universe at any moment of time; here, "self-fulfillment" is defined as an intensity of beauty and harmony greater than the sum of its parts.[2]

From this perspective, God's initial aim for Jesus and Jesus' subjective for himself were, as my Buddhist friends have it, "non-dual." Or as David Ray Griffin writes, "We may think of Jesus' structure of existence in terms of an 'I' that is co-constituted as

2. Whitehead, *Process and Reality*, 108, 224–44.

much by divine agency within him as by his own personal past."[3] This means that the normal tensions between God's initial aim and the purposes received from the past—which express our subjective aims to achieve our own self fulfillment—did not exist in the historical Jesus—at least after his sojourn in the desert. This, in turn, created openness to God's call in each moment of Jesus' life. Whereas, in the language of the Prologue to the Gospel of John, the Word or *logos* is incarnated in all things and events—in every human being—Christians can reasonably affirm that the historical Jesus is the Christ of faith because God's incarnation in the form of God's initial aim for Jesus constituted his very selfhood.

Consequently, the historical Jesus was fully human. But for whatever reason, he conformed his subjective aim for himself to God's initial aim for him: not my will but "your will be done," as the Lord's Prayer has it (see Matt 6:5-14). One can reasonably conclude that while the Word, in the form of God's initial aim, is incarnated in all things and events, the historical Jesus became the Christ of faith by completely identifying his subjective aim for himself with God's initial aim for Jesus. Or to cite the words he is reported to have said on the night before he was crucified, "Not my will, but your will be done" (see Mark 14:32-42). In my view, the historical Jesus was no different than any other human being because, in the language of the Nicene Creed, "he was made man." But in the union of his subjective aim for himself with God's initial aim for the historical Jesus he was in non-dual harmony with God, or in the language of the Gospel of John, with the *logos* incarnated in all things and events (John 1:1-18), and became the Christ of faith. In this man's life and death, human beings meet, that is, apprehend God within the conditions of historical existence. This is why everything "Christian" starts with the Incarnation, even as most incarnational doctrines are incoherent. A process understanding of Christian experience of the Incarnation—that the historical Jesus is the Christ of Faith—removes the incoherencies of classical Christology.

---

3. Cobb and Griffin, *Process Theology*, 105.

12

Unqualified Disciples

I recently heard a sermon on Matthew 9:35—10:8. The narrative of this text revolves around Matthew's list of the twelve disciples. Mark and Luke also identify the twelve disciples by name, and despite slight variations in Matthew's, Mark's, and Luke's lists they have one glaring feature in common: not one woman's name appears. The closest a woman comes to appearing in any list of disciples is in Acts 1, where Luke appends—perhaps as a last-minute thought—the comment that "certain women," including Jesus' mother, joined with the twelve disciples after their trip to Jerusalem.

The omission of women from the list of disciples hardly comes as news. As feminist biblical scholars truthfully point out, every text in the Bible assumes patriarchal assumptions about the relationship between men and women. But here is what interests me: the way in which Matthew's, Mark's, and Luke's silence about female disciples has been transformed into a legal precedent—particularly by the more conservative Protestant traditions, Roman Catholicism, and the Christian right. Using an ecclesiastical alchemy, the story in which Jesus authorizes the ministry of a handful of his followers becomes a timeless law restricting leadership in the church to men. By confusing this gospel text for a legal precedent, we could equally conclude from this story that being a Christian has little to do with feeding the hungry—since Jesus does not specifically mention it in these verses—and that only Judeans should hear the proclamation of the gospel—since the twelve disciples are sent only to "the lost sheep of the house of Israel."

But there is always more than one way to skin a biblical text. So instead of reading this story as a set of legal precedents, we can concentrate instead on several very provocative anomalies. For example, there's the tension between Jesus' observation that the crowds are like sheep without a shepherd and his declaration that more laborers are needed for the harvest. Apparently, the sheep require shepherds that are to be drawn from the sheep. Jesus' observation—that the crowds are like sheep in need of leadership—arises from compassion. Compassion is what happens when we experience the utter interdependence of all life so that the suffering of one human being is the suffering of all human beings. Thus, Jesus instructed the disciples, who are part of the flock of sheep they are to lead, to cure the sick, raise the dead, cleanse leapers, and cast out demons—a set of instructions that evokes images of the Kingdom or Commonwealth of God that is present, but not fully, and ascribes to the twelve disciples a prophetic role. The disciples are instructed to become both shepherds and prophets, but how these two tasks are related is unclear.

A second interesting anomaly arises from the act of sending out the twelve disciples as missionaries. Notice that Jesus announces the need for workers, then summons the twelve disciples and gives them a set of instructions. But nothing in the text indicates that they go anywhere. In the corresponding story in Mark and Luke, the twelve disciples actually leave, and when they return they report to Jesus about their experiences. But Matthew says nothing about this. My guess is that the explanation for this anomaly has something to do with the didactic or "educational" nature of Matthew's gospel. Most of the Gospel of Matthew is an extended instruction on discipleship; if the disciples are waiting for the "Great Commission" to go out into the world and make

Unqualified Disciples

disciples of all human beings, the disciples' actual departure lies beyond the confines of Matthew's account of the historical Jesus. Two more features make these anomalies even more curious. Jesus gives the twelve disciples conflicting assignments, as anyone who has tried to be both prophet and shepherd very quickly learns. In more Lutheran language, what we have here are two conflicting "calls." And despite the intentionality with which Jesus sends out the disciples to be both shepherds and prophets, they do not appear to leave for their mission. I mean, what qualifies any of the twelve disciples for the title "apostle"—meaning "someone who is sent out to perform a task," in this case, a prophetic task? The point is that Matthew doesn't bother explaining what qualifies the twelve disciples for their apostolic mission.

There are no clues to these anomalies in the text itself. We do not learn anything about the twelve disciples that compose Jesus' inner circle other than their names, and in a few cases the identity of a brother or father, and a rather vague geographical reference. The two exceptions make the question about the disciples' qualification even more odd and perhaps a bit amusing: Matthew is identified as a tax collector and Judas as "the one who betrayed him." I wonder if this was Judas's call, but that's another question.

Tax collectors were social lepers in Jesus' day and were always regarded as dishonest collaborators with the Romans. Tax collectors had an even lower reputation in the ancient world than they do in ours, and the phrase "tax collectors and sinners" says it all. Identifying Judas as Jesus' betrayer not only hints at the passion narrative that comes later in Matthew's Gospel, but also provides an unmistakable signal that even those in Jesus' immediate circle cannot understand who he is—or what he represents—or the meaning of his teachings until after his Crucifixion. There is nothing in the list of the twelve disciples that indicates how Judas or Matthew or anyone else qualifies to be a disciple.

So, here's the thing. No one is qualified to be a disciple. An earlier scene in the fourth chapter of Matthew in which Jesus calls some fishermen to follow him, and again his call to other men in chapter 9 provide not the slightest hint that these men were special

Faith as Remembering

or had special skills, other than some were fishermen and tax collectors. In fact, nothing in any of these passages tells us what led Jesus to choose this group of men over any other group. They didn't apply for the position. They submitted no resumes that listed their training and areas of expertise. There were no letters of recommendation supporting an application for the position "disciple." They are merely "authorized, but never "qualified."

In the sixties rock opera, "Jesus Christ Superstar," there is a scene in which the disciples engage in a bit of wine-enhanced conversation during the Last Supper. They talk about their hopes of making it as apostles, and they imagine becoming famous in their old age by writing gospels and being remembered after their deaths. The first time I saw this scene I laughed so hard I couldn't stop. Someone even sent for an usher to ask me to leave—which I did not. See, the church has indeed preserved the memory of the disciples, and the humor lies in imposing an achievement ethic onto a story that refuses to be read as another "how to succeed manual."

Therefore, I sometimes wonder if Christians who hear Matthew's Gospel read, or who read it themselves, are sufficiently aware of conditions. I mean just think of the implications. I suppose we could read this story as a legal text and come up with some sort of Canon law to justify the practice of ordaining only those who prove themselves fit for ministry—only tax collectors and traitors need apply. Such a rule would be as ridiculous as excluding women from ministry because their names do not appear in the list of Jesus' disciples.

But here's where the text gets rather bumpy: only the unqualified can present themselves. Just as no one—absolutely no one—was qualified to be an apostle, no one—absolutely no one—is qualified for undertaking the various forms of Christian faith and practice. No one is qualified for God's graceful call to faith. No one, not a single human being. Or in a slightly different paraphrase of St. Paul's teaching, no one is "justified by faith through qualifications alone." Anyone—back in Jesus' time or today—who serves as the twelve disciples did does so by Jesus' authorizing call that is oblivious to qualifications, which throws us back to the text's central feature: the historical Jesus as the Christ of faith is the one who actually heals as he sends never-qualified disciples into the world in his name.

What do these textual anomalies say about us, two thousand years later? I must confess that my exegesis or interpretation of this gospel text probably sounds like how a scholar teaching New Testament in a university or seminary setting might approach any biblical text. In fact, I've used the methods of literary criticism and other critical methods to try to understand biblical texts in their own historical contexts my whole professional life, which is never an easy thing to do. My suspicion is that anyone reading this chapter is asking, "so what?" I also suspect that readers already know the answer to this "so what?" question.

Like the original disciples, all persons following the Christian Way are unqualified. Like the original disciples, Christians are called to discipleship that takes no heed of our qualifications. Responding to the call to discipleship is faith, meaning trust in God in place of our own "qualifications." But here's the hiccup. As Dietrich Bonhoeffer wrote in *The Cost of Discipleship*, when God calls a person, God calls that person to his death. Not always a literal physical death, but always the death of our individual egos. Faith is a way God starts a fight with us, and discipleship may be very costly.

Bonhoeffer was right. Discipleship is socially engaged faith active in love on behalf of the poor, in the struggle for gender and environmental justice, in dialogue with the world's religious Ways, in dialogue with the natural sciences, in the political rough-and-tumble to create compassionate and just communities, which means giving to people what people need for meaningful existence. Discipleship is working for peace by confronting the religious, political, and economic domination forces that promote the violent oppression of whole communities. Discipleship is what goes on in our own circumstances, always unqualified, always struggling to understand what our callings are, always making mistakes, sometimes fearful, sometimes brave, very often creative beyond our own wildest imaginations, in community with other unqualified disciples throughout the church trying to do the same thing. In other words, we are sheep and shepherds simultaneously.

13

Religious Pluralism

In an excellent book on the lives of four Catholic writers—Dorothy Day, Thomas Merton, Flannery O'Connor, and Walker Percy—Paul Elie cogently describes the structure of the postmodern experience of religious diversity.

> We are all skeptics now, believer and unbeliever alike. There is no one faith, evident at all times and places. Every religion is one among many. The clear lines of orthodoxy are made crooked by our experience, and are complicated by our lives. Believer and unbeliever are in the same predicament, thrown back onto ourselves in complex circumstances, looking for a sign. As ever, religious belief makes its claim somewhere between revelation and projection, between holiness and human frailty, but the problem of proof, indeed the burden of belief, for so long upheld by society, is now back on the believer, where it should be.[1]

If Elie's description is an accurate one, certain implications follow that will serve as working assumptions about the structure of the experience of religious pluralism:

---

1. Elie, *The Life You Save May Be Your Own*, 472.

- "Pluralism" is not just another name for "diversity." Pluralism goes beyond naming the fact of the existence of differing religious Ways. Pluralism goes beyond mere diversity to active theological engagement with the plurality of religious Ways. We can study diversity, celebrate it, or complain about it, but diversity alone is not pluralism.

- Pluralism is an attitude, a theological orientation, dare I say, a theoretical construct. Given the strong universalism of traditional Christian claims about the historical Jesus as the Christ of faith, any theology of religions, of which pluralism is one option, is strictly a Christian enterprise. Non-Christians do not encounter religious pluralism as a problem in the same way that Christians encounter religious pluralism as a problem.

- Pluralism is not an ideology, nor a Western neo-liberal scheme, nor a debilitating form of relativism.[2] Pluralism is best understood as a dynamic process through which we dialogically engage with one another through our very deepest differences. As usual, I shall appropriate the metaphysics of Whiteheadian process philosophy as a means of conceptualizing pluralism as dynamic process.

- Pluralism as a theoretical construct is not mere tolerance of "the other," but an active attempt to understand "the other." Pluralism is a theological-philosophical move beyond tolerance based on exclusivist and inclusivist theologies of religions toward constructive understanding of what to make of the empirical facts of religious diversity.[3]

---

2. See the collection of essays edited by Gavin D'Costa, *Christian Uniqueness Reconsidered*. Each contributor to this volume, in varying ways, argues that pluralist theologies of religions are in fact forms of debilitation relativism and thereby an expression of intellectual imperialism that reduces the diversity of the world's religious Ways to a particular worldview, thereby committing what Whitehead called the "fallacy of misplaced concreteness," and therefore are fundamentally ahistorical.

3. See Ingram, *Wrestling with the Ox*, ch. 2; and Ingram, *The Modern Buddhist-Christian Dialogue*, ch. 2, for my critique of contemporary exclusive and

- Pluralism is not debilitating relativism. It does not displace or eliminate deep religious or secular commitments. On the contrary, pluralism is the *encounter* of commitments. Many critics of pluralism persist in linking pluralism with a kind of valueless relativism, in which all perspectives are equally compelling and, as a result, equally uncompelling. Pluralism, they contend, undermines commitment to one's own religious Way with its own particular language by watering down particularity in the interests of universality. I consider this view a distortion because pluralism is engagement with, not abandonment of, differences and particularities. While encountering people of other faiths may lead to a less myopic views of one's own faith, pluralism is not premised on a reductive relativism.

- The language of pluralism is dialogue—vigorous engagement, and argument are essential in a democratic society. Dialogue is vital to the health of religious faith so that we appropriate our faith not by habit or heritage alone, but by *making* it our own within the context of conversation with people of other religious Ways. Dialogue is aimed not at achieving mere agreement, but at achieving relationship. Dialogue as the language of pluralism is the language of engagement, involvement, and participation.

- As a theoretical construct, pluralism is never a completed project, but the ongoing work of every generation.

A suggestive model for imagining the structure of religious pluralism can be appropriated from Imre Lakatos' description of the structure of scientific research programs. Lakatos' most influential essay is titled "Falsification and the Methodology of Scientific Research Programs,"[4] in which he described the actual practice of science in terms of competing research paradigms, rather than

inclusive theologies of religious.

4. Lakatos and Musgrave, eds., *Criticism and the Growth of Knowledge*, 91–96.

as a historical series of complex competing paradigms, as it is for Thomas Kuhn.[5]

Lakatos described some of these research programs as "progressive" and others as "degenerating." A degenerating research program is one whose core theory is "saved" by ad hoc modifications that form a protective belt—mere face-saving devises or linguistic tricks—meant to protect the core theory from criticism. As Nancey Murphy points out, it is difficult to know what "ad hoc modifications" mean since it is always difficult to propose criteria for determining what these non-scientific face-saving modifications are.[6]

Lakatos was clear, however, on the conditions necessary for a progressive scientific research program. First, each new version of the theory—what he called its core theory and its hypotheses—preserves the unrefuted content of its predecessor, for example as Einstein's general and special theories of relativity preserved the unrefuted content of Newtonian physics. The function of the core theory is to unify the program by providing a general view of the nature of the entities being investigated. Second, this theoretical core is surrounded by a "protective belt of hypotheses," which function as lower-level theories that support the core theory. Also included here are theories of instrumentation and statements of initial conditions. Third, there must be empirical data that support both the core theory and the hypothesis. When the first and second conditions are met, a scientific theory is said to be theoretically progressive. When all three conditions are met a research program is also empirically progressive.[7]

Since in the actual practice of the natural sciences deductive reason based on hypotheses make explanation and confirmation symmetrical, the hypotheses nearest the data being researched explain the data, as higher-level hypotheses explain lower level

---

5. Murphy, *Theology in the Age of Scientific Reasoning*, 58–61. Also see Kuhn, *The Structure of Scientific Revolutions*.

6. Murphy, *Theology in the Age of Scientific Reasoning*, 59.

7. Ibid., 59–60. Also see Murphy and Ellis, *On the Moral Nature of the Universe*, 11–13.

theories, while the core theory is the ultimate explanatory principle for all data. For this reason, Lakatos described the auxiliary hypotheses as a "protective belt," since potentially falsifying data are accounted for by making changes at the level of the auxiliary hypotheses rather than in the core theory, which he called the "hard core" because it cannot be abandoned without abandoning the entire research program, as illustrated in the figure A below. Thus, a progressive research program is fundamentally a temporal series of networks of theory, along with supporting data, in which the hardcore stays the same but the auxiliary hypotheses change over time to account for new data and the data's relation to the research program's "hard core.

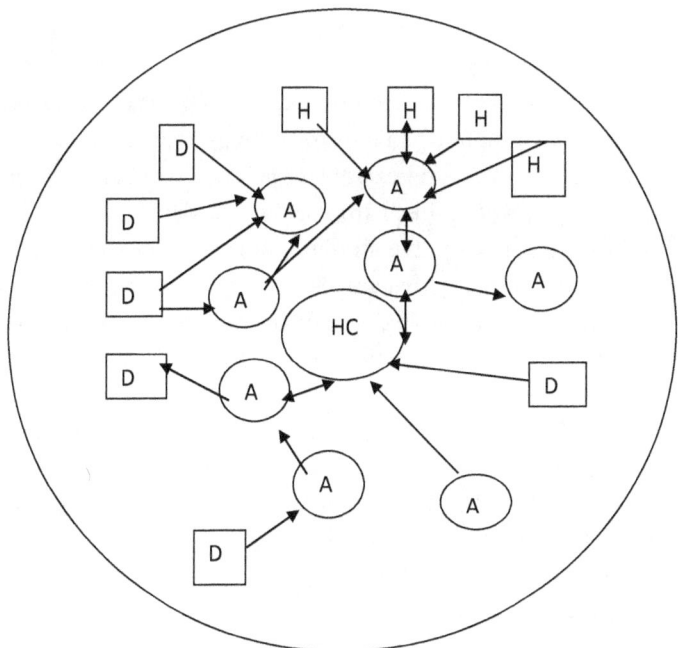

Figure A: Structure of a Scientific Research Program

A progressively mature scientific research program also involves what Lakatos called a "positive heuristic," which is a plan for systematic development of the program to take account of broad arrays of new data. This reflects the recognition of the role of models in contemporary philosophy of science. Scientists employ a wide variety of models, for example the double helix model of DNA and other mathematical and physical models of various sorts. The function of a positive heuristic is to envision the development of a series of increasingly accurate models of the processes and entities under scientific investigation. For example, the hard core of Isaac Newton's research program consisted of his three laws of motion and the law of gravitation as influence at a distance. The auxiliary hypotheses included initial conditions and applications of the three laws of motion and gravity to specific problems. The positive heuristic included working out increasingly sophisticated explanations for the orbits of planets: first calculations for a one-planet system with the sun as a point-mass, then solutions for more distant planets.

Murphy argues that scientific research programs as described by Lakatos can be applied directly to theology as an academic discipline.[8] As one of several examples she cites Wolfhart Pannenberg's theology, where the "hard core" is his claim that the God of the historical Jesus is the all-determining reality. This is Pannenberg's central theory that guides the development of his entire theological program. Like a scientific research program, the positive heuristic of any systematic theology like's Pannenberg's is to engender theories ("auxiliary hypothesis") that meet the following conditions: (1) they are faithful to authoritative pronouncements within particular faith communities; (2) they elaborate or spell out the content of the hard core in a way that (3) relates a community's doctrines to available data (sacred texts, the authoritative teaching of a community evolving over time, the experiences of participants in a community). In Pannenberg's example, the hard core—that God is the all-determining reality—requires that "data" include not only biblical texts, but facts and theories from all areas

---

8. See Murphy, *Theology in the Age of Scientific Reasoning*, ch.6, for examples of other theological research programs as well as an outline of her research program.

of knowledge, including the natural sciences interpreted through the hard core of his research program.

Theological pluralism can also be viewed as a research program. The simple fact of religious diversity, John Hick writes, in itself raises no serious theological issues. "It is only when we add what can be called the basic religious conviction that a problem is generated."[9] By "basic religious conviction," Hick meant the conviction that our religious beliefs, practices, and experiences are not illusions because they refer to a transcendent reality which he called "the Real." Whether such convictions are justifiable is one of the central issues of philosophy of religion. But Hick's point is that all religious persons claim that their beliefs and practices bear ontological reference to a transcendent reality, named and experienced differently within the contexts of humanity's various religious traditions. This constitutes the "hard core" of Hick's pluralist hypothesis and my notion of pluralism as a research program.

Most often, according to Hick, the basic religious conviction carries an additional claim: one's particular religious tradition is the most valid response to "the Real" because it bears an ontological correspondence to "the Real" missing from religious traditions other than one's own. But can such claims—which most participants in all religious Ways assert—ever be validated? I think they cannot since the wider religious life of humanity occurs within the limits imposed by historical and cultural experience. For Hick, this means that no one can know the Sacred "as such" but only as mediated through the filters of history, tradition, and culture.

It is this philosophical reading, Kantian in its epistemological assumptions, that leads Hick to posit the pluralistic hypothesis: if (1) the basic assumption of humanity's religious traditions is the existence of an absolutely transcendent and real reality (the hard core), then (2) all of humanity's religious traditions can be understood as "auxiliary hypotheses," meaning "different ways of experiencing, conceiving, and living in relation to an ultimate divine reality which transcends all particular visions of it."[10] Accordingly,

9. Hick, *God Has Many Names*, 88.
10. Hick, *An Interpretation of Religion*, 237.

different forms of religious experience that engender different teachings, practices, and images are not necessarily contradictory or competitive in the sense that the truth of one entails the falsehood of the other, although often this is the case. In Hick's understanding, each religious tradition reflects encounters with "the Real" within the context of their individual historical and cultural perspectives.

Hick's pluralist hypothesis has been sharply, and perhaps unjustly, criticized for establishing the truth of multiple religious traditions by reducing them to a single common element that asserts that the religions of the world are essentially identical at their cores. In fact, this is not Hick's claim. He understands perfectly well the diversity of the truth claims in the world's religions. A Kantian epistemology might allow one to take such an ahistorical position. But Kantian as he is, Hick does not draw this conclusion. The "hard core" of his theory is that the religious traditions of humanity embody historical experience of an "ultimate reality," which he calls "The Real." His auxiliary hypotheses do not reduce the historical complexity of the world's religions to a single common element.

My contention is that objections to Hick's pluralist hypothesis can be met by (1) appropriating Lakatos' model of how scientific research programs actually function, and (2) reformulating the pluralist hypothesis in terms of Whiteheadian process thought. The "hard core" of my research program agrees with Hick: all religious traditions reflect culturally and historically limited experiences of a reality that transcends them all and that they all seek to describe this reality according to their own traditions. But this reality is incredibly complex and what the religious traditions of the world teach about this reality are not identical; their teachings and practices are not identical even though they are referencing the same sacred reality. Instead, each individual religious Way expresses truths intended to be universal, but not the full truth. That is, the specific religious Ways of the world constitute a series of auxiliary hypotheses intended as true accounts of reality, meaning the way things really are as opposed to the way we want things to be, even though the teachings and practices of the world's religious Ways are often similar, often different, sometimes contradictory, and occasionally complementary in their differences.

In this reformulation, the world's religious Ways potentially express truth claims that either complement or contradict each other. This assumes that different religious Ways address aspects of the human condition relative to their individual cultures and histories, so that attention must be paid to these differences. Thus, for example, Buddhist concepts of Awakening and Christian concepts of salvation are different and express different experiences of the Sacred. But by understanding the differences and raising questions in dialogue, Buddhists and Christians can mutually enrich their own unique understandings of reality.

The primary mode of theological reflection supported by the pluralist research program I am proposing is interreligious dialogue, which is portrayed in figure B below. Understanding what I mean requires an explanation of the diagram using a number of bullet points.

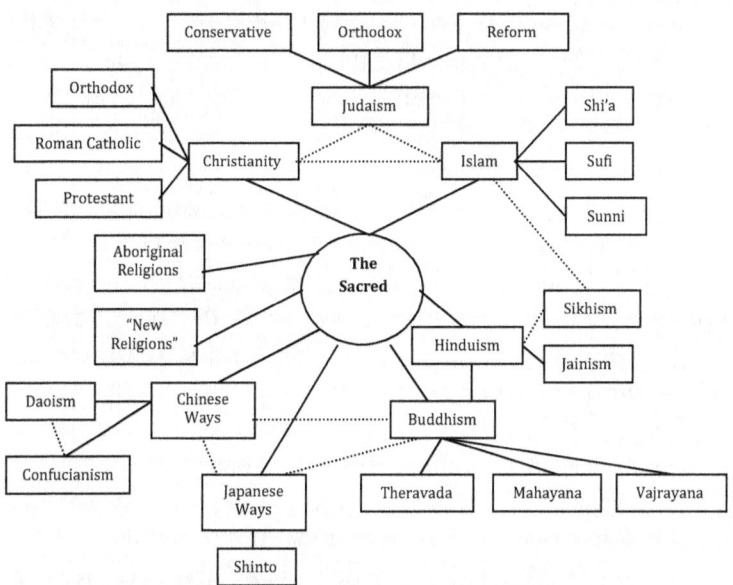

Figure B: Model of a Pluralist Research Program

Faith as Remembering

- According to Alfred North Whitehead, "creativity" is "the category of the ultimate," meaning "the universal of universals characterizing ultimate matters of fact," a process by which "the universe disjunctively becomes the one actual occasion, which is the universe conjunctively." In the process, "the many become one and are increased by one."[11] As metaphysically ultimate, all things and events, in Whitehead's language all actual occasions of experience and societies of actual occasions of experience, at every moment of space time—past, present, future—are particular forms of this universal creative process, including God, whom Whitehead believed was the chief example of the creative advance. As metaphysically ultimate, creativity has no boundaries, which is symbolized in Figure B by the empty spaces occupied by the circle and the boxes.

- The center of the diagram is occupied by a circle upon which I have written "The Sacred," and which John Hick calls "the Real." Of course, the Sacred is not limited by conventional "boundaries" since according to Whitehead, God is ingredient in the becoming of all things and events in the creative advance of the universe. My choice of "the Sacred" to designate the central referent in the diagram reflects my training in history of religions. Although it is open to criticism, "the Sacred" seems an appropriate descriptive designation of the referent of religious experience wherever it occurs. Thus, while I intend to employ this term generically I also realize that as neutrally as I try to employ it, "the Sacred" carries explicit Western and perhaps even Christian theistic connotations which may not be fully adequate to the experiences of non-theistic religious persons. Even so, provided we are sensitive and careful, the term can be employed as a general designation for the referent of religious experience, practice, and traditions. While I realize that this idea is open to the charge that it posits a "common ground" that often creates a

---

11. Whitehead, *Process and Reality*, 31–32.

Religious Pluralism

debilitating relativism because it explains by explaining away real religious diversity and difference, persons who make this claim also invest themselves in interreligious dialogue. How this dialogue is possible without reference to a sacred reality that transcends all religious Ways—however it is named—is often not clear.

- Accordingly, anyone who affirms interreligious dialogue as a theological practice tacitly implies that there is a common referent to which the collective religious Ways of humanity point, and it serves no purpose to deny it.[12] This constitutes the "hard core" of my pluralist research program. The specific problem is how to indicate this common referent more specifically without explaining away the real convergences, incommensurablities, and diversities that constitute pluralism of the world's religious Ways.

- The boxes surrounding the circle bear the name of some of the major religious Ways. I have included the best-known Ways and have left others out, i.e., Zoroastrianism, because I wanted to keep the diagram as simple as possible, yet still specify the theoretical structure of my research program. In actual practice, one would have to include Zoroastrianism since its monotheism is historically connected to Jewish, Christian, and Islamic monotheism. My intention is to portray the various religious Ways as "auxiliary hypotheses" which form the "protective belt" surrounding the hard core. Each box is connected to the Sacred by an unbroken line representing my hypothesis that each of humanity's religious Ways refer to real but historically and culturally limited experiences of the Sacred. The implication is that no individual religious Way can claim either universal validity or absolute truth about the Sacred to which they all refer.

- The broken lines linking Judaism, Christianity, and Islam are meant to indicate that these monotheistic Ways have

---

12. For a more complete response to the criticism of "common ground" notions of religious pluralism, see Ingram *Wrestling with the Ox*, 172–74.

shared history, culture, teachings, and practices. The broken lines linking Islam with Sikhism and Hinduism with Sikhism represents the origins of Sikh tradition in Guru Nanak's teachings, which sought to harmonize aspects of Islam and Hinduism into a synthesis as a means of overcoming Hindu-Islamic violence. The broken lines linking the Chinese Ways and the Buddhist Way and Chinese Ways and Japanese Ways indicate the influence of Buddhist tradition in Chinese religious thought and practice in such movements as Neo-Confucianism, as well as the influence of the Buddhist Way in the religious history of Japan and its influence on Shinto and as the primary vehicle by which the Confucian and Daoist Ways were imported to Japan. The broken line linking the Daoist and Confucian Ways indicate the fact that in the experience of most Chinese persons, the Daoist and Confucian Ways do not function as separate traditions. Finally, the broken line linking Shi'a, Sunni, and Sufi forms of Islam indicate that these three forms of Islam share the defining character of the practice of Islam for all Muslims, the intention to "surrender" to the will of God, as well as the fact that Sufism is practiced within both Sunni and Shi'a communities.

- The boxes surrounding the major religious traditions represent various sub-traditions within each of the major religious Ways. Thus Orthodox, Conservative, and Reform traditions of the Jewish Way are themes and variations on two thousand years of Jewish history and experience. Orthodox religious experience, Conservative religious experience, and Reform religious experience constitute the "data" supporting Jewish teaching about the Sacred and its practices. Likewise, Orthodox, Roman Catholic, and Protestant forms of the Christian Way constitute the "data" supporting two thousand years of Christian experience of the Sacred, as Sunni, Shi'a, and Sufi experience constitute "data" for the truth and practice of fourteen hundred years of Islamic monotheism. The Daoist, Confucian, and Buddhist Ways provide the "data" supporting Chinese religious experience, while Theravada, Mahayana, and Vajrayana traditions are data supporting Buddhist teachings and practices.

- By "data," I mean the religious experience of persons who participate in the various movements within the major religious traditions throughout their histories. Of course, scientific data and the data of religious experience are not identical. For one thing, the data that support scientific theory are public, experimentally repeatable, closely tied to theory expressed mathematically, and are more-often-than-not unrelated to ordinary human experiences of the world. The data of religious experiences, while closely related to doctrines and teachings, are not experimentally repeatable, and carry a subjectivity not easily, if ever, open to empirical observation in the way that physical "facts" seem to be in the natural sciences. Nevertheless, the data of religious experience supports the teachings of the various religious Ways as differing referents to the Sacred. Otherwise, persons would not be practicing these Ways.

I think the experience of God as incarnated in the historical Jesus as the Christ of faith is the main push toward a pluralistic theology of religions for Christians. This push originates from two essential characteristics of Christian experience of God: mysterious and trinitarian. There is also a third push: historical consciousness that relativizes all knowledge.[13] Our knowledge of anything, including knowledge of God, is limited by the cultural and historical points of view we occupy at the moment we claim we know anything. If this is true, historical consciousness also teaches us that the reality of God that Christians apprehend incarnated in the historical Jesus as the Christ of faith is not limited by what Christians apprehend. Consequently, while historical consciousness tells us that every glimpse of truth we can have is intrinsically finite and conditioned, "religious consciousness"—religious experience contextualized by the historicity of all knowledge—tells us that God is more than any human being can grasp.

13. Hick, *God Has Many Names*, 88.

Consequently, Christian religious experience has a paradoxical edge: any historical encounter with God is as mysterious as it is real, as ambiguous as it is reliable. Mystics and non-mystic theologians who have sensed and urged this recognition of God as utter mystery populate the history of Christian tradition: St. Paul, Augustine, Thomas Aquinas, Julian of Norwich, Marguerite Porete, Meister Eckhart, Martin Luther, John Calvin, John Wesley, and most recently, Karl Rahner, Edward Schillebeekx, Thomas Merton, Paul Tillich, Karl Rahner, Daniel Day Williams, Paul Knitter, John Cobb, and others too numerous to name.

But to affirm that we cannot know *everything* about God does not mean that we cannot know *something*. The paradox that sits at the heart of Christian faith and practice is the incarnation: in the life, death, and resurrection of a human being two thousand years ago in a backwater region of the Roman Empire, humanity encountered God within the realities of historical existence. No question. Or in the words of Luther's *Small Catechism*, "This is most certainly true." But while the historical Jesus reveals God, the incarnation does not reveal all that God is. I deeply suspect that most Christian talk of the incarnation as "God in human form" or the "fullness" of the divine mystery in the historical Jesus or the Christian right's unqualified assertion that "Jesus is God" tends to violate the meaning of the incarnation than preserve it. Affirming the incarnation does not mean that the historical Jesus took on all that constitutes God or that God took on all that constitutes being human. Accordingly, while the historical Jesus, as the Second *persona* of the Trinity, defines who God is for Christians, Jesus does not exhaust what God is. To ignore the limitations of the incarnation is to fall into docetism—the heresy that stresses the divinity of Jesus as it denatures his humanity. Much popular and fundamentalist Christian theology is docetic.

Consequently, perceiving God's incarnation in the historical Jesus is simultaneously recognizing that God cannot be limited to the historical Jesus. The reality Christians encounter in Jesus is truly available and found beyond Jesus, as Edward Schillebeekx never tired of pointing out.[14] No religious Way, therefore, has the final or the exclusive or the inclusive word about God. Final words limit and demystify God and are more useful for the politics of power in Church hierarchies than relevant to the religious needs of faithful Christians. Final words are, as Wilfred Cantwell Smith never tired of pointing out, forms of idolatry—*shirk* in Islamic formulation, meaning reducing God to that which is not God and surrendering to it.[15] An idol is not something that mediates God to faithful persons, but something that seeks to confine God to a series of theological propositions or a liturgical system or a book or an institution claimed to be the final mediator of God.

When one reflects carefully about it, the reality Christians name "God" cannot be confined to any one religious tradition because the reality of God—that which constitutes God as God—is both unity and plurality. I agree with Paul Knitter that this is the deepest content of Christian experience symbolized by the doctrine of the trinity:[16] God is one and God is plural, which, as it turns out, can be conceptualized in the categories of process theology. God's "primordial nature," meaning God's self-identity through the moments of God's time, is what God always is as God, beyond the categories of thought and always in interdependent relationship with the universe God continually creates as the First Person of the Trinity (the "Father").[17] Yet the primordial nature of God is always in non-dual interdependency with the "plurality" of God's "consequent nature"—God as God mutually affects and is affected

---

14. Schillebeeckx, *The Church*, 184.
15. Smith, *Faith and Belief*, ch. 3.
16. Knitter, *Jesus and the Other Names*, 38–39.
17. "Father" is in parentheses because while this is traditional Christian usage, it is troublesome because of its sexist overtones. "Father" is an inadequate designation of God as the creator and sustainer of the universe. One could use "Mother" or both, depending on what one wishes to theologically stress, and both would adequately, but incompletely, point to Christian experience of God. In my theological reflections, I sometimes think of God as Mother, sometimes as Father, sometimes and both—Mother and Father. For a concise description of this aspect of Trinitarian theology, see Cobb, *Christ in a Pluralistic Age*, 259–64.

by all things and events in the universe throughout the moments of God's experience—two thousand years ago through the Second Person (the Son) and before and after the death of Jesus through the Third Person (the Holy Spirit). God in God's primordial nature needs "manyness" to be God in God's consequent nature.

My point is not that God has one nature inadequately expressed in different religious traditions, although this seems to me to be true. My point is that there are real and genuine differences within what medieval Christian mystics called "the Godhead" and what process theology calls God's primordial nature and God's continuous interaction with the universe and the great variety of human communities that constitute God's consequent nature. As Whitehead noted, since God cannot be an exception to the metaphysical principles through which God creates the universe, plurality seems essential to reality from subatomic particles to religious traditions to God. Metaphysically, this means that the principle of interdependence is at the heart of existence. Accordingly, just as God cannot be reduced to a unity that would remove the differences between the three persons of the Trinity, so Christians can trust that the plurality of the world's religions Ways cannot be reduced to the kind of unity that would remove the real differences among the various religious Ways in order to prove the superiority of one Way and the inferiority of the rest.

God's character as unconditioned love is modeled for Christians by the historical Jesus as the Christ of faith. Christians are thereby called to unconditionally love all human beings and the creatures of God's creation as God unconditionally loves all human beings and the creatures of God's creation, with no ego strings attached. Such love is not detached, but passionately involved. We are all brothers and sisters because the existence of all creation originates from God. We should therefore relate to one another according to what is needed, which may often be different from what is wanted. In this sense, love is "non-personal": like rain falling on the earth, God's love falls on all without regard to social status, economic influence, or merit, so don't take it personally. Yet the interdependent flip side of unconditional love is justice, which according to the prophetic tradition out of which Jesus lived and taught is liberation from all institutional and personal obstacles that cause suffering and prevent persons from achieving what they need for meaningful life in community with one another, with nature, and with God. Love as the non-violent struggle for justice for all persons as well for all other sentient beings is involved and passionate.

Consequently, for Christians love of God—the first commandment—engenders the second commandment: unbounded love directed by compassionate wisdom that takes priority over all other ethical injunctions, religious practices, theological systems, and institutional demands. The second commandment means loving one's neighbor and has priority over proclaiming doctrine or formally worshipping God. The New Testament standard is this: first work out things with your neighbor, brother or sister, then go to church or synagogue or mosque or temple (Matt 5:23-24). Don't allow religious practices, with its professions of doctrines and ritual observances to get in the way of doing good for your neighbor. It's better to break the Sabbath than to fail in loving your neighbor (Matt 12:12).

Viewed from the role loving compassionate wisdom played in the faith and practice of the historical Jesus, there is something fundamentally wrong with traditional Christian views of other religions. For starters, to practice loving compassionate wisdom means engaging non-Christians in dialogue not as "other" but as persons who in mutual interdependence with us seek truth. In dialogue, we listen to our non-Christian brothers and sisters with real openness to what they are saying. Dialogue means treating them as we would want them to treat us. It means listening to their witness to truth as we would want them to listen to ours. It means confronting them when we think they are wrong, even as we must be ready to be confronted by them when they think *we* are wrong. In short, to love one's neighbors wisely and compassionately means to be in dialogue with them.

However, traditional Christian attitudes toward the world's religion Ways—both the inclusive and exclusive models—are obstacles to treating neighbors with love in dialogue. An exclusive model interprets all religious Ways different from one's own as false. Persons participating in these "other" Ways are in error and in need of conversion to one's own Way. An inclusive model asserts that whatever truth exists in a religious Way other than one's own is a partial reflection of the full truth of one's own religious Way.[18] So persons participating in these Ways are not in complete error, but are in need conversion to one's own Way to be in full contact with saving truth. Both models contradict the practice of loving, compassionate wisdom.

For me, as a Christian monotheist, the questions are these: can we respect our non-Christian brothers and sisters and be open to them if we must believe before we even meet them that our truth is better than theirs, that they are inferior to us in what they hold to be true and sacred? And can we affirm and love them when we are convinced with *a priori* certainty that they must agree with our truth if they are going to arrive at the fullness of God's truth? Whenever we hold up a truth claim and insist that according to God's will it is the only and absolutely final "truth" by which all other truths must be measured, then it is impossible to relate to them as our brothers and sisters. While absolutizing the Christian Way into a universal norm for measuring all religious claims does enable us to confront non-Christians as "other," it does not allow us to encounter them or be encountered by them as brothers and sisters, as loving compassionate wisdom requires.

Finally, I think there is growing awareness among many Christians—both in the pews of churches and among theologians—of a discrepancy between theological reflection and ethical practice. This conflict lies between the view of non-Christian Ways asserted by traditional exclusive and inclusive Christian beliefs and teachings and the conduct toward non-Christian persons required by Christian ethics—an ethics that can only be based on loving compassionate wisdom if it is Christian.

---

18. For an analysis of several versions of theological exclusivism and inclusivism, see Ingram, *Wrestling with the Ox*, ch. 1.

Essentially, the conflict many Christians experience is between theological orthodoxy—right beliefs—and orthopraxy—right behavior.[19] Partly this has to do with the fact that as more Christians have come to know non-Christians, it has become clear that our non-Christian brothers and sisters are in general neither less nor more kind, thoughtful, loving, wise, or compassionate than are Christians.[20] Increasingly, Christians are experiencing tension, if not contradiction, between the first and second commandments and the final commandment of Christian faith—to spread the Gospel to all nations as they extend love to all human beings and the creatures of the Earth with compassionate wisdom. While Jesus instructed his disciples to love their neighbors as themselves, he is also said to have given them third commandment—to go forth into the world and make his message known to all human beings. Christians are called upon to love their neighbors and to make the good news about Jesus known so as make disciples of all human beings.

Again, in Luther's language, "This is most certainly true." Yet for whatever reason Christians have tended to make this third commandment more important than the first and second commandments, or at least the criterion for practicing the first and second commandments, throughout Christian history. Christians have spread the Gospel throughout the world but have all too often not loved their non-Christian brothers and sisters wisely or compassionately in the process. Given the inclusive and exclusive models for understanding the third commandment, Christians have frequently not respected, listened to, learned from, or affirmed their non-Christian neighbors as loving compassionate wisdom requires.

---

19. Knitter, *Jesus and the Other Names*, 40–45.

20. In this regard, my experience is similar to Hick's. "My own inevitably limited experience ... has led me to think that the spiritual and moral fruits of these faiths, although different, are on a par with the fruits of Christianity; and reading some of the literature of the different traditions, both some of their scriptures and philosophies and some of their novels and poetry portraying ordinary life, has reinforced this impression." Hick, *A Christian Theology of Religions*, 12–16.

Faith as Remembering

The theological and ethical contradictions between the first and second commandments and the last commandment, between Christian ethical *praxis* and Christian doctrine, between orthopraxy and orthodoxy has a long history. However, given the priority of the orthopraxy of loving one's neighbor as oneself wisely and compassionately over the orthodoxy of theological doctrine—as modeled by Mark's account of the historical Jesus—exclusive and inclusive models for understanding our final commission should be rejected and replaced by the practice of interreligious dialogue guided by loving compassionate wisdom. It's not that theological reflection is unimportant. Theology is, after all, "faith seeking understanding," as St. Anslem put it in the eleventh century. But doctrinal orthodoxy is not more important than the practice of unbounded love and compassionate wisdom. For like everything else in the universe, the practice of loving compassionate wisdom and theological reflection are interdependent.

14

A Meditation on Environnemental Destruction[1]

According to the natural sciences, there is continuity between organic and inorganic structures, which means there exists a fundamental continuity between human and nonhuman life as embodiments of these structures. Alfred North Whitehead underscored this continuity by including "higher animals" in his definition of "living person"; human beings and animals are living persons characterized by a dominant occasion of experience that coordinates and unifies the activities of the plurality of occasions and enduring objects that ceaselessly form persons and animals over time. Personal order is linear, serial, object-to-subject inheritance from the past in the present. Personal order in human beings and nature is one component of what Whitehead called "the doctrine of the immanence of the past in the present." This linear, one-dimensional character of personal inheritance from the past is the "vector-structure" of natural processes. A similar picture of nature is ingredient in the Daoist concept of *de* (power) and

1. This chapter is a slight revision of a post I wrote titled "Daoist–Buddhist–Christian Dialogue: A Reflection on Environmental Destruction" for the websites jesusjazzandbuddhism.org and processphilosophy.org, both edited by fellow process theologian, Jay McDaniel.

Hua-yin (Flower Wreath) Buddhist interpretations of the doctrine of interdependent causation.

But the question is, "So what?" Part of the answer is, I think, because what people do to the natural environment corresponds to what people think and experience about themselves in relation to the natural events surrounding them. This may seem obvious to philosophers, theologians, and scientists. But it is not so obvious when attention shifts from theoretical issues to empirical confirmation of our worldviews in actual human practice.

Three facts require consideration. First, the brute fact of global environmental destruction seems to imply that what people think does not substantially affect what they do and how they live. Second, in a world shrunken to a global village by communication and transportation technologies, multinational corporations, and nuclear weapons, pointing to non-Christian views of nature as a means for resolving the ecological crisis may not even be an option. As the world is now increasingly organized, "development" and "progress" mean "industrialization." Industrialization, even when pursued in a climate of anti-Western ideology, means becoming economically Western. Third, technology is neither cultural-neutral nor value-neutral. To adopt contemporary technology means simultaneously adopting the values in which that technology is immersed. Contemporary technology is grounded in a Baconian-Newtonian-Cartesian complex of ideas—science as manipulative power over inert lumps of dead matter.

But as brutish as these facts are, the present environmental crisis is also less a unique, unprecedented event than the continuation of events as old as pre-Occidental and pre-Oriental civilization. All life forms modify the environment. Human beings are not exceptions. What *is* exceptional about the human species is that's our stratagem for survival and adaptation—culture—has not only amplified the environmental impact of human beings on nature, but also to a large degree has placed us in charge of our own evolution and perhaps our extinction. Consequently, it is

A Meditation on Environnemental Destruction

imperative that we choose to live harmoniously with all sentient beings "before it's too late," as John Cobb has it.[2]

This is so because even at the level of empirical confirmation of scientific theory, it seems evident that the destruction of the natural processes supporting all sentient beings is directly related to the psychological and spiritual health of the human species cross culturally. Culture and worldview, faith and practice merge in human language and indicate perceptions in persons and in societies of persons. When we relate to nature as a thing separate from ourselves or as separate from God, we not only engender, but also perpetuate the environmental nightmare through which we are now living. The Christian word for our separation from God and nature is "sin." The Buddhist word is "desire" (*tanhā*). The Islamic word is "idolatry" (*shirk*).

Accordingly, quite apart from problems of cultural and theological redirection, our immediate goal should be to preserve whatever biological diversity we can. The human species need not be a blot on the environment or a burden to other sentient beings. For as Daoist and Buddhists views of nature and Whiteheadian process thought confirm, human beings can actually enhance the diversity, integrity, stability, and beauty of life on this planet. An irresponsible, technologically exploitative human civilization informed by a scientifically obsolete, reductionist, mechanistic worldview is not the only possibility, provided we give this planet a chance to cease rushing like lemmings over a cliff toward global destruction.

But the environmental destructiveness of Western rationalism's hyper-*yang* view of its own culture is still running full steam ahead. The ecological limits of the Earth are now stretched and, in some cases, broken. But dialogue with the Daoist and Buddhist Ways might foster a process of Western self-critical consciousness raising by providing alternative places to stand and imagine new possibilities. Engaging in such a dialogue requires understanding that we neither stand against nor dominate nature.

2. Cobb, *Is It too Late?*

But like any dialogue, a Daoist–Buddhist–Christian dialogue, with the natural sciences as a fourth partner, has an inner and outer dimension. Discussion of organic paradigms must not remain at the level of verbal abstraction. Daoists and Buddhists can understand and appreciate the language of Christian process views; process theologians can understand and appreciate Daoist and Buddhist teachings and practices. In dialogue, Daoists, Buddhists, and Christians may be creatively transformed. But this is an example of conceptual dialogue. Important as such dialogue is, it is incomplete if divorced from an interior dialogue about how Daoists, Buddhists, and Christians can personally experience non-duality between themselves and nature. For to the degree we experience the realities to which Daoist, Buddhists, and process Christian concepts of nature point, to that degree we are energized to live in accord with the organically interdependent structures of nature that conceptual dialogue reveals.

It's like the union of lyrics with music in a great chorale: the music of interior dialogue enfleshes the abstract lyrics of conceptual dialogue. What interior dialogue teaches is that we can live any way we want. People take vows of poverty, chastity, and obedience—even silence—by choice. People destroy the environment by choice, because they experience it as a lifeless thing. But choosing to experience nature organically is to stake our calling in skilled and supple ways, to locate the tenderest spot in nature we can find and plug into its pulse. This is yielding to nature, not dominating nature.

From a Daoist or Buddhist perspective transformed by encounter with Christian process thought, conceptual and interior dialogue mean, to paraphrase Joseph Campbell, following our collective bless. Would it not be proper, and obedient, and pure to begin by flowing with nature rather than dominating nature, dangling limp from nature wherever nature takes us. Then even death, where we are going no matter what, cannot us part. Seize nature and let it seize us up aloft, until our eyes burn and drop out. Let our murky flesh fall off in shreds, and let our bones unhinge and scatter, loosened over fields and wood, lightly, thoughtless,

A Meditation on Environnemental Destruction

from any height at all, from as high as eagles. Then we discover that there was never anything to seize, nothing to grasp all along, because we are nature looking at ourselves.

Or from a Christian process theological perspective transformed by conceptual and interior dialogue with the Daoist and Buddhist Ways: God does not demand that we give up our personal dignity, that we throw in our lot with random people, that we lose ourselves and turn from all that is not God. For God is the "life" of nature, *intimor intimo meo*, as Augustine put it, "more intimate than I am with myself." God needs nothing, demands nothing like the stars. It is life with God that demands these things. Of course, we do not have to stop abusing the environment—unless we want to know God. It's like sitting outside on a cold, clear winter's night. We don't have to do so; it may be too cold. If, however, we want to look at the stars, we will find that darkness is necessary. But the stars neither require nor demand it.

15

The Pluralism of Life and Death

Sometimes when I think about death and dying, usually when I'm alone late at night, thoughts revolve inside my head like wheels within wheels. It's a bizarre feeling because the problem with thinking about death is that we don't know what we're thinking about, an experience analogues to what mystics tell us about God-talk: when we talk about God, we don't know what we're talking about. Of course, we certainly know *that* death is, that it will happen to every living thing. But we do not know *what* death is because before we can know anything, we must first experience what we know. But by the time we experience our death, it may be too late to know the experience.

Years ago on a sullen November day I took hike in the foothills of the High Sierras that ended at a forgotten cemetery. The weather was threatening, but I was driven by an unusual restlessness. Snow covered the land like a white shroud and clung to the pine trees like cotton by the time I reached the cemetery bathed in gray twilight. The community that placed it there had long vanished. Season by season, frost, snow, and summer's heat had cracked the flat headstones until none remained upright. As I stood freezing among the frozen dead I saw the only other living thing in this bleak place—a mule deer showing ribs. Only the

The Pluralism of Life and Death

storm contained us. That shrinking, long-eared animal cowering helplessly beside a slab in an abandoned graveyard expected the momentary flash of death. But it did not run. And I, with a rifle I used to carry in that day and time, also stood while snow—a real blizzard by then—raged over and between us. But I did not fire, and have not fired since.

We had the power to be fruitful and multiply, I remember thinking. Why was it so, and what was the message that somehow seemed wordlessly spoken from a long way off, carried by the cold and the wind, out of explicit human hearing? The wind swirled snow around us as the temperature fell. The mule deer needed that bit of shelter. In its trembling body, in the millions of years of evolution between us, there was no storyteller's aid. It had survived alone, thin and emaciated. But it was alive and that was triumph enough.

I slowly backed away from the mule deer and the dead human beings and their fallen gravestones. I knew that if I could follow the fence lines, there would be a fire and company for me. But then I suddenly knew: it was out of such desolation that all life forms had arisen, and to such desolation that all things caught in the field of space-time will return. We are in essence belated ghosts of an angry winter searching for springtime.

The mule deer was another of my many "hidden teachers," as Loren Eiseley phrased it, and it taught me four lessons. First, the rules of evolution require death; life grows out of death; death generates life. Sentient beings must eat other sentient being to survive. Life demands killing, and all sentient beings live on the death of other sentient beings. Death seems to be the necessary condition energizing the evolutionary processes creating life wherever life happens in the universe.

Second, there seems to be one commandment shared by all species: survive. Species are armed for survival, fanged for it, timid for it, hungry for it, fierce for it, clever for it, intelligent for it. This commandment decrees the suffering and death of myriads of individuals for the survival of the whole. Life has one final end: to be alive. All the tricks and mechanisms, all the evolutionary successes and failures, are aimed to this end. It seems to be the natural order of things that the pluralistic processes of death sustain and support the plurality life.

Third, the interdependency of life and death is a "natural fact of existence." It is neither cruel nor merciful. True, death can often seem to come as a welcomed friend bringing release from suffering. Yet death is a reality that directly challenges any religious Ways teachings and practices.

Finally, as if this were not enough, human beings, nature's top predator, add to the pluralism of suffering and death required by evolutionary processes. We are one of the few species that kills other species for reasons other than food. We also kill each other, in extreme instances motivated by rationalizations we invent to justify war, racial hatred, religious imperialism, gender oppression, and oppression of the poor by the wealthy and politically powerful.

So here lies the hard truth. The only species that is a blot on nature, with the ability and will to push the forces of death beyond death's natural capacity to support life, to the point of extinguishing all life on this planet, is also the one species that most intimately knows the terror of death, that experiences most acutely the rip that death creates in the human community and humanity's community with non-human life. So even as human beings have killed or been killed or have died "naturally," sometimes in suffering, sometimes not, our species is haunted by a question: "Is this all there is?" The religious Ways of humanity, in a pluralism of ways, all assert that there is more than this, that there is much more than death. I cannot think of a stronger justification for the practice of interreligious dialogue centering on this "more" than this.

The plurality of quests to discover if death is ultimately "all there is" is a religious exploration of how value can be maintained at the limits of life without seeking illusory compensation. Stated more theologically, this is the soteriological ground upon which the religious Ways of humanity, each in their own distinctive ways, explore the universal human capacity for self-delusion and the recognition that life yields to life, part to part. The attainments of the

The Pluralism of Life and Death

whole, whether it be in forms of life on a coral reef or human life in a city, seem to demand a sacrifice few sentient beings are willing to make, but which some nevertheless do, thereby marking their deaths for the well-being of the whole.

The theme of sacrifice is perhaps the earliest category through which humanity's Religious Ways explore the nature and significance of death. Sacrifice is fundamentally not simply life yielding death to give continued meaning to life. It is the religious exploration of death in all its pluralism that brings us to more sensitive awareness of evil. How we think about death and the processes of dying flows back and forth like a möbis strip into our moral, aesthetic, and political decisions while we are alive.

But it is equally true that the many different views of the possibility of transformation beyond death cannot all be true. All may be false, but they cannot all be true, at least as propositions about matters of fact. Certainly, propositional differences in the soteriologies of humanity's Religious Ways are important to those who believe them. These propositions are not trivial, in the way that a preference for yellow, say, rather than green might be. For example, Jews and Muslims agree that human beings are teachable: we can follow God's instructions recorded in the Torah or the Qur'an about how to live in community. Thus, the Jewish and Islamic Ways might be said to have relatively optimistic views of human nature. But the Christian Way is relatively pessimistic about human nature; subversive egoism and evil lie at the root of every human enterprise and we cannot be educated into salvation. "Salvation," whatever this means, if it is to come at all, comes *in spite of* who we are. Or if one is a Lutheran, "by grace alone."

Still, the propositional differences between humanity' religious Ways in relation to death—their pictures of death and what may or may not survive it—may be approximate yet mainly wrong. They may also be wrong yet approximate about some fundamental demand arising from human experience. In this sense, the pictures and concepts of different religious conceptualities may reinforce each other, even though in their conceptual details they are incommensurable. This does not mean that issues of truth disappear; it is simply that truth issues are not foreclosed in advance. Choices remain to be made, far short of immediate verification or falsification since in the nature of the case verification cannot be other than eschatological.

This is why I find myself driven back to the theme of sacrifice as the affirmation of the value and worth of the entire universe, which cannot exist on any other terms than death. Affirming that death is a necessary condition for new and creative transformations of life is the heart of the religious category of sacrifice. Each of the religious Ways of humanity affirms sacrifice in this sense. What we learn from this is that we must love the universe and our life—along with the life of all sentient beings—while not clinging to anything with attachment, as my Buddhist friends say, because here, as Christians might say, we have no abiding city—because "he is not here. Why seek the living among the dead?" (Luke 24:5).

For Christians, the life, death, and resurrection of the historical Jesus confessed to be the Christ of faith constitutes the single event that initiates new life created through his sacrificial death, a new life we are now able to live in the here-and-now if only incompletely. For Mahayana Buddhists, it is through the enlightened sacrificial compassion of numerous Bodhisattvas that we can realize transformed life beyond death's entropy. Both Christian and Buddhist affirmations of the necessity of sacrifice for the creation of new life mean that in a universe like ours, creative transformation requires death as the cost we, and God, if one is a Christian process theologian, must pay for transformed life.

Therefore, in the between time of our own births and deaths, we discover life through interrelationships—with nature, with each other, with the poor and oppressed struggling for liberation—here and now. Making the struggle for liberation in all its forms our struggle—which it is in an interdependent universe—requires that we focus on the life we are living in the midst of death, here and now.

Still, I have a suspicion. The struggle for the liberation of life, for the liberation of women and men from patriarchy, for the liberation of the poor and the oppressed, requires a special kind of

The Pluralism of Life and Death

death of the self, a death we can experience while alive. The death of self of which the religious Ways of humanity speak is not a violent act. It is merely joining with the universe in its roll. It is merely the cessation of the ego's willful spirit and the intellect's chatter. It is waiting like a hollow bell with stilled tongue, for whatever might come. It's the waiting that's the thing, because not only does life come if we wait; we discover that it has been here all along, pouring grace over us like a waterfall.

Then we understand what Annie Dillard meant when she wrote that there is always an enormous temptation "to diddle around making itsy-bitsy friends pursuing itsy-bitsy needs and making itsy-bitsy journeys for years on end until we die."[1] We should not have any of this. The necessity for sacrifice will not allow us to be so conventional, because the universe is wilder than this in all directions, more extravagant and bright, more dangerous and bitter. "We should never make hay when we can make whoopee; we should never raise tomatoes when we should be rising Cain or Lazarus."[2]

Thus, as a Whiteheadian-Lutheran historian of religions and process theologian, I have come to think that the category of sacrifice reveals that not only is there grace operating in the processes of life and death, but there are also very few guarantees. To be sure, our *needs* are guaranteed, absolutely guaranteed—for liberation—but by the strictest of warranties, in the plainest language: "knock, seek, ask." But as the New Testament and Annie Dillard warn, we had better read the fine print: "I do not give to you as the world gives" (John 14:27).

For me, the meaning of the beginning and ending of existence for all things and events caught in the field of space time is most meaningfully portrayed in the Gospel of Mark's account of the historical Jesus' argument about the resurrection of the dead: "As for the dead being raised, have you not read in the book of Moses, in the passage about the bush, how God said to him, 'I am the God of Abraham, the God of Isaac, and the God of Jacob?'

---

1. Dillard, *Pilgrim at Tinker Creek*, 269.
2. Ibid.

He is not God of the dead, but of the living" (Mark 12:26-27a). In other words, God did not abandon the Hebrew patriarchs once they served their purpose, but has an eternal destiny for them. Likewise, God does not abandon the universe and its life forms after they have served their purpose.

But how credible is such hope given what physics and biology continually reveal about the physical processes of the universe? Although there exist strands of Christian tradition that affirm the survival of an immortal soul-entity after death, I think the traditions that come closest to what the natural sciences reveal about the natural order is the New Testament's vision of hope of resurrection beyond death. In this context, the issue is not one of surviving death because of the existence of an immortal soul or self-entity remaining self-identical through time. My understanding of selfhood is influenced by Buddhist notions of non-self that seem to me highly congruent with Biblical notions of selfhood and Whiteheadian process philosophy's account of selfhood. All three affirm that neither the human self nor other sentient forms of selfhood are permanent. Existence is characterized by impermanence because of the Second Law of Thermodynamics. In this, Buddhist teaching, biblical tradition, and process theology are in full agreement with the natural sciences.

According to Whitehead, the human self and the selves of whatever other life forms experience degrees of conscious self-awareness is a complex, dynamic, information-bearing pattern that is physically embodied at any instant in the complex societies of actual occasions that constitute the physical body. Each "self" exhibits its own "subjective aim" to achieve the maximum fulfillment of which it is capable, given the physical and historical contexts in which it finds itself and which it must take into account. But the self is also "lured" by God's "initial aim" that its own "subjective aim" be in harmony with God's aim that all entities achieve their own final fulfillment or "satisfaction" in interdependence with all occasions aiming to achieve *their* "satisfaction." In the complex life form that is a human being, the self's subjective aim and God's initial aim are usually in conflict, but both operate

The Pluralism of Life and Death

in the self's becoming. According to John Cobb, what made the historical Jesus so extraordinary was that Jesus' subjective aim and God's initial aim for Jesus were non-duel.[3] Or in traditional Christian language, the historical Jesus subordinated his will for himself to God's will for the historical Jesus. In this regard, this is the reason Muslim tradition—the Qur'an and the Sunna—portray the historical Jesus as a "Muslim," one who "surrenders to God's will."

The psychosomatic unity of the self's physical embodiment is dissolved at death. But I think it is coherent to hope that the pattern that is me, as well as the pattern of all living things, from the moment of conception to the moment of death, is remembered—in Whitehead's word, "prehended"—and reconstituted by God in a new environment of God's choosing, which is what I understand to be the meaning of St. Paul's notion of resurrection:

> What I am saying, brothers and sisters, is this: flesh and blood cannot inherit the Kingdom of God, nor does the perishable inherit the imperishable. Listen, I will tell you a mystery. We will not all die, but we will be changed, in a moment, in the twinkling of an eye, at the last trumpet. For the trumpet will sound, and the dead will be raised imperishable, and we will be changed. (1 Cor 15:50–52)

In other words, life is embodied in physical processes; all life is embodied life. Whatever hope can reasonably exist that death is not all there is lies in the resurrection of the body. By this I do not mean the resuscitation of our present physical structures. In physicist-theologian John Polkinghorne's "crude analogy":

> The software running on our present hardware will be transferred to the hardware of the world to come. And where will that eschatological hardware come from? Surely the "matter" of the world to come must be transformed matter of this world. Hence the importance to theology of the empty tomb, with its message that the Lord's risen and glorified and body is the transmutation of his dead body . . . It is in the resurrection of Jesus that the destiny of humanity and the destiny of the universe

---

3. *Christ in a Pluralistic Age*, 97–110.

together find their mutual fulfillment in a liberation from decay and futility.[4]

Polkinghorne's image of cosmic redemption in which a resurrected humanity will participate is "as immensely thrilling as it is immensely mysterious."[5] Still, such an unimaginable future reflects an almost universal hope that, all the ambiguities and suffering of history notwithstanding, in the end, all will be well. Historically, such hope is so widely prevalent as to constitute what Peter Berger called a "signal of transcendence."[6] I think it is important that Christians not lose their nerves in witnessing to this "signal."

Accordingly, in the community of faith called the church, Christians know the present for what it is—a point of time too charged with eternity to be understood except through mythic and poetic language. By this I mean language drawn from biblical imagery, two thousand years of theological reflection, the experience of worship, art, music, social engagement, and in our day and time, the practice of interreligious dialogue. It is the only way we can reflect on that which we have not experienced while we are alive. The problem is that no one alive knows *what* death, only *that* death is, because we can only know anything by rational reflection on what we know by experience. But by the time we experience *our* death, it may be too late to reflect rationally on the experience.

The need to employ mythic and poetic language in order to speak about what we have not yet experienced must not create the illusory comfort of fables. For Christians, this means betting one's life on, that is, trusting, being faithful to, the historical Jesus as the Christ of faith. Such faith need not imply that only Christians experience resurrection or that, whatever resurrection is, it occurred for the first time in history at the resurrection of the historical Jesus. David Toolan expresses this point this way:

---

4. Polkinghorne, *The Faith of a Physicist*, 164.
5. Ibid.
6. Berger, *A Rumor of Angels*, 72–76.

The Pluralism of Life and Death

> In hindsight, the church has understood Jesus in cosmic terms. As the New Testament testifies, Jesus has to be taken as the prototype of our species and, better yet, in cosmic-ecological terms, as the archetype of what quarks and molecules, from the beginning, were predestined to become—one resurrected body. Jesus is not simply a moral example. He is, as St. Paul would have it, the axis of cosmic time and the prototype of the fullest embodiment of our species' role: the carrier and vessel, the fleshing out of the Creator's great dream for the universe.[7]

The two primary sources for Toolan's conclusions are St. Paul and the Gospel of John. For both creation has a central importance. As the Gospel of John has it, "In the beginning was the Word, and the Word was with God and the Word was God . . . and without him [God] was not anything made that was made." (John 1:1–3). Both the writer of the Gospel of John and St. Paul concluded that the creation of the universe entails redemptive salvation. Or, to put it in another way, creation and redemptive salvation are interdependent. To the original followers of the Jesus Way, this must have sounded as if God's Torah or "instructions" had surfaced in the words of a man, because in hearing the historical Jesus they apprehended the voice of the Creator. The primordial Word was "made flesh, he lived among us, and we saw his glory . . . full of grace and truth." (John 1:14) In other words, the central Christian claim is that two thousand years ago a minority of one in a backwater region of the Roman Empire altered the course of the universe's history.

However, if God is ultimately the source of all that is because the laws of nature originated with God, the reality of evil and suffering becomes a central problem for not only Christian faith and practice, but also humanity's sister monotheistic Jewish and Islamic Ways. It's rough out there in the universe where the survival of any life form entails the suffering and death of countless species. Life *must* eat life to survive. Furthermore, human beings have brought suffering not only to other human beings but to

---

7. Toolan, *At Home in the Cosmos*, 208.

nature itself. Suffering is real—for all sentient beings—and those suffering know it.

For Christian theological reflection, the question is: if God's power is best understood and experienced as love—Whitehead would say that God's power works as a divine "lure" that "persuades" all things and events to achieve their fullest "satisfaction" as all things and events contribute to the ongoing creative process and simultaneously to God's own experience—then God is not a cosmic tyrant who predestines events before they happen. Love for God and for us happens in relationships, none of which are permanent, that recognize the independence and interdependence of that which is loved.

In other words, from electrons to human beings, God structures freedom into the universe itself. Freedom may be trivial at the sub-atomic level, but for human beings and other sentient beings it is not. We are free to reject God's lure to live in mutually interdependent fulfillment with one another and with nature, which means that God will not stop a murderer from shooting a weapon or prevent the Holocaust or genocide in places like Rwanda. Here, Luther's "theology of the cross" provides important insights: God interacts with the word, shares the world's suffering with us, and redeems what can be redeemed from the mess we make as well as from the suffering that the processes of evolution naturally entail. But God does not control everything because love means allowing the beloved freedom not to respond to love that is offered.

At this point, the natural sciences can again inform theological reflection. The more physics and biology reveal about the universe, the more the universe looks like a packaged deal. While human beings make creative contributions to the creative process even as we add to the natural suffering already ingredient in life, we also tend to believe that if we were in charge of the universe we would keep all the good and throw away the bad. But neither the universe nor anything else can be divided so dualistically. For example, contemporary biological theory shows how genetic mutation has driven the evolutionary history of life on this planet, eventually transforming bacteria into human beings. Genetic

The Pluralism of Life and Death

mutation is a great good, but this same process allows some cells to become malignant; the evolution of life cannot happen without cancer, which causes untold suffering for millions of people.

Freeman Dyson notes something similar. "There is a "sloppiness" to life, he writes, "in which life must be able to tolerate error in order to be robust. Novelty happens at the edge of chaos, so that if something is too stable, it's just rigid and nothing new can happen. But if something is too chaotic it falls apart. "It's in that edge, that sloppy region where openness is joined to preservation that life really happens." This region is a necessarily dangerous place, not because God is careless or in incompetent. "It's just the cost of the fullness we call life."[8]

I think something like this idea lies behind St. Paul's portrayal of the historical Jesus as the Christ of Faith:

> He is the image of the invisible God, the first born of all creation; for in him all things were created, in heaven and earth, visible ad invisible . . . he is the beginning, the first born from the dead, that in everything he might be permanent. For in him all the fullness of God was pleased to dwell, and through him to reconcile to himself all things, whether in earth or in heaven. (Col 1:15–20)

Or as John Cobb interprets the structure of experience of Christian faith:

> The structure of experience with Christ which is bound up with hope in history is that of dying and rising. Each moment, as soon as it is realized, itself perishes or dies. The new moment truly lives only as it finds some novel possibility that is its own, appropriate to its unique situation, and worthy of realization in its own right. Living from our past instead is not a real option. If we seek life by clinging to past realizations of it, we do not live at all. It is only a question of the pace of death. The one who holds to the past and repeats it does not enliven the past but only joins it in death. However, the one who turns from the past to openness to the new finds the past restored

---

8. Dyson, concluding paragraph.

and revitalized . . . It is when we think new thoughts that our past thinking remains a vital contributing element, not when we endlessly repeat ourselves or try to defend what we thought in the past.[9]

In other words, it is by dying that we live. Whatever redemption is, it encompasses more than humanity, past, present, or future; redemption encompasses the whole natural order, every thing and event in the universe since the first instant of the Big Bang until the physical processes of this universe finally play out trillions of years into the future. For as St. Paul put it, "God was in Christ reconciling the world to himself" (2 Cor 5:19). The deepest meaning of the universe, the meaning of 13.7 billion years of evolution and beyond, is that all of nature, every thing and event caught in the field of space-time—past, present, and future—is always united with God. Nothing is left out that can be included. Absolutely nothing.

---

9. Cobb, *Christ in a Pluralistic Age*, 243.

Bibliography

Berger, Peter. *A Rumor of Angels: Modern Society and the Recovery of the Supernatural*. Garden City, NY: Doubleday, 1969.
Bonhoeffer, Deitrich. *The Cost of Discipleship*. 2nd rev. ed. New York: Macmillan, 1995.
Borg, Marcus. *Meeting Jesus Again for the First Time: The Historical Jesus and the Heart of Contemporary Faith*. San Francisco: HarperSanFrancisco, 1994.
Bratzlaw, Nathan. *The Golden Mountain*. New York: Berhman House, 1991.
Cobb, John B., Jr. *Christ in a Pluralistic Age*. 1975. Reprint, Eugene, OR: Wipf & Stock, 1999.
———. *Is It too Late? A Theology of Ecology*. Denton, TX: Impact Books, 1995.
Cobb, John B., Jr., and David Ray Griffin. *Process Theology: An Introductory Exposition*. Philadelphia: Westminster, 1976.
D'Costa, Gavin, ed. *Christian Uniqueness Reconsidered: The Myth of a Pluralistic Theology of Religions*. Faith Meets Faith Series. Maryknoll, NY: Orbis, 1990.
Dillard, Annie. *Teaching a Stone to Talk: Expeditions and Encounters*. New York: Harper & Row, 1982.
———. *Pilgrim at Tinker Creek*. New York: Harper & Row, 1985.
Dyson, Freeman. *Origins of Life*. Rev. ed. Cambridge: Cambridge University Press, 1999.
Elie, Paul. *The Life You Save May Be Your Own: An American Pilgrimage*. New York: Farrar, Straus & Giroux, 2003.
Hanson, K. C., and Douglas E. Oakman. *Palestine in the Time of Jesus: Social Structures and Social Conflicts*. 2nd ed. Minneapolis: Fortress, 2008.
Hedrick, Charles W. *The Wisdom of Jesus: Between the Sages of Israel and the Apostles of the Church*. Eugene, OR: Cascade Books, 2014.
Hick, John. *A Christian Theology of Religions*. Louisville: Westminster John Knox, 1995.
———. *God Has Many Names*. Philadelphia: Westminster, 1982.
———. *An Interpretation of Religions*. New Haven: Yale University Press, 1989.
Ingram, Paul O. "Daoist–Buddhist–Christian Dialogue: A Reflection on Environmental Destruction." http://jesujazzbuddhism.org/daoist-buddhist-

Bibliography

christian-dialogue-a-reflection-on-environmental-destruction.html. (May 2016).

———. *The Modern Buddhist-Christian Dialogue.* Lewiston, NY: University Press of America, 1988.

———. "To John Cobb: Questions to Gladden the Atman in an Age of Pluralism." *Journal of the American Academy of Religion* 45/2 Supplement (1977) 763–88.

———. "On Seeing, Scripture, and Tradition." http://processphilosophy.org/on-catching-glimpses-of-the-sacred.html (October 2015); and http://jesusjazzbudhism.org/on-catchng/glimpses-of-the-sacred.html (October 2015).

———. *Theological Reflections at the Boundaries.* Eugene, OR: Cascade Books, 2012.

———. *You Have Been Told What Is Good: Interreligious Dialogue and Climate Change.* Eugene, OR: Cascade Books, 2016.

———. *Wrestling with God.* Eugene, OR: Cascade Books, 2006.

———. *Wrestling with the Ox: A Theology of Religious Experience.* 1997. Reprint, Eugene, OR: Wipf & Stock, 2006.

Keller, Catherine. *Cloud of the Impossible: Negative Theology and Planetary Entanglement.* Insurrections: Critical Studies in Religion, Politics, and Culture. New York: Columbia University Press, 2014.

Knitter, Paul F. *Jesus and the Other Names: Christian Mission and Global Responsibility.* Maryknoll, NY: Orbis, 1996.

Kuhn, Thomas S. *The Structure of Scientific Revolutions.* Chicago: University of Chicago Press, 1970.

Lakatos, Imre, and Alan Musgrave, eds. *Criticism and the Growth of Knowledge.* Studies in Logic and the Foundations of Mathematics. Cambridge: Cambridge University Press, 1970.

Murphy, Nancey. *Theology in the Age of Scientific Reasoning.* Cornell Studies in the Philosophy of Religion. Ithaca, NY: Cornell University Press, 1990.

Murphy, Nancey, and George F. R. Ellis. *On the Moral Nature of the Universe: Theology, Cosmology, and Ethics.* Theology and the Sciences. Minneapolis: Fortress, 1996.

Niebuhr, Reinhold. *The Nature and Destany of Man.* 2 vols. New York: Scribner, 1943. 2nd ed., 1964.

Norris, Kathleen. *Amazing Grace.* New York: Riverhead, 1998.

———. *The Cloister Walk.* New York: Riverhead, 1996.

Oakman, Douglas E. *Jesus and the Peasants.* Matrix 4. Eugene, OR: Cascade Books, 2008.

———. *The Political Aims of Jesus.* Minneapolis: Fortress, 2012.

Polkinghorne, John. *The Faith of a Physicist: Reflections of a Bottom-Up Thinker.* Minneapolis Fortress, 1996.

Porete, Marguerite. *The Mirror of Simple Souls.* Translated and introduced by Ellen I. Babinsky. Classics of Western Spirituality. New York: Paulist, 1993.

Bibliography

Schillebeeckx, Edward. *The Church: The Human Story of God*. Translated by John Bowden. New York: Crossroad, 1990.

Smith, Wilfred Cantwell. *Faith and Belief*. Princeton: Princeton University Press, 1979.

Tillich, Paul. *Systematic Theology*. Vol. 1, *Reason and Revleation. Being and God*. Chicago: University of Chicago Press, 1951.

Toolan, David. *At Home in the Cosmos*. Maryknoll, NY: Orbis, 2001.

Welty, Eudora. *One Writer's Beginnings*. William E. Massey, Sr. Lectures in the History of American Civilization 1983. Cambridge: Harvard University Press, 1984.

Whitehead, Alfred North. *Process and Reality: An Essay in Cosmology*. Gifford Lectures 1927/28. Corrected ed. Edited by David Ray Griffin and Donald W. Sherburne. New York: Free Press, 1985.

Wright, N. T. *The Day the Revolution Began: Reconsidering the Meaning of Jesus's Crucifixion*. New York: HarperOne, 2016.

Index of Names

Abe, Masao, 59
Adams, Fred, 42
Anselm of Canterbury, 11, 112
Aristotle, 84
Augustine, Saint, 20, 78, 106, 117

Barth, Karl, vii
Berger, Peter, 126, 131
Black Elk, 64
Bonhoeffer, Deitrich, 20, 75, 91, 131
Borg, Marcus, 74, 76, 131
Bratzlaw, Nathan, 37, 131
Buddha, 5, 55–59, 69, 82

Calvin, John, 106
Cobb, John B., Jr., 4, 11, 34, 36, 47–49, 86, 106–7, 115, 125, 129–31
Confucius, 5, 69
Constantine, 22

Dalí, Salvador, 18
Davis, Bette, 15
Dawkins, Richard, 42
Day, Dorothy, 93
D'Costa, Gavin, 94, 131
Descartes, René, 3–4, 12, 47
Dillard, Annie, 9, 13, 123, 131
Dyson, Freeman, 129, 131

Eckhart, Meister, 50
Einstein, Albert, 96
Eiseley, Loren, 9, 27, 119
Elie, Paul, 93, 131
Elijah, 63
Eliot, T. S., 18
Ellis, George F. R., 132
Emerson, Ralph Waldo, 9, 18
Ezekiel, 68

Francis of Assisi, St., 36

Gandhi, Mahatma, 18
Griffin, David Ray, 85–86, 131

Hadewijch of Antwerp, 50
Hanson, K. C., viii, 76, 131
Hedrick, Charles W., 70, 131
Hick, John, 99–100, 102, 105, 111, 131
Hubbell, Edwin, 41
Huntington, Ronald M., 55

Ingram, Regina Ruth (Inslee), 8, 11
Ingram, Paul O., 11, 15, 20, 29, 48, 62, 67, 76, 94, 103, 110, 131–32
Inslee, Robert Ray, 8–9

Index of Names

Jesus, 8, 5, 18, 20–26, 30–32, 34, 36, 39, 44, 51, 57, 59, 67–91, 94, 98, 105–9, 111–12, 122–23, 125–27, 129
John the Baptist, 79
Judas, 89
Julian of Norwich, 106

Keller, Catherine, 48, 132
Khan, Badshah, 26
King, Martin Luther, Jr., 18, 26
Knitter, Paul F., 106–7, 111, 132
Kuhn, Thomas S., 96, 132

Lakatos, Imre, 95–98, 100, 132
Luther, Martin, 2, 9, 31, 53–54, 78, 106, 111, 128

Matthew, 89
McDaniel, Jay B., 113
Mechthild of Magdeburg, 50
Melville, Herman, 9
Merton, Thomas, 28–29, 93, 106
Mohammed, 5, 83
Murphy, Nancey, 96, 98, 132
Murray, Cecil, 26
Musgrave, Alan, 95, 132
Myōkō, Naganuma, 59

Newton, Isaac, 98
Nichiren, 59
Nikkyō, Niwano, 59
Niebuhr, Reinhold, 82, 132
Norris, Kathleen, 35–36, 132

Oakman, Douglas E., viii, 76, 131–32
O'Connor, Flannery, 9, 93

Pannenberg, Wolfhart, 98
Pārvati, 62

Paul, Saint, 20, 24, 34, 44–45, 78, 80–81, 90, 106, 125, 127, 129–30
Peary, Robert Edwin, 13
Percy, Walker, 93
Perlmutter, Saul, 40–41
Picasso, Pablo, 18
Plato, 84
Polkinghorne, John, 125–26, 132
Pontius Pilate, 80
Porete, Marguerite, 49–55, 69, 106, 132

Rahner, Karl, 106
Ross, Floyd H., 4

Sagan, Carl, 56
Śankara, 83
Schillebeeckx, Edward, 106–7, 132
Schmidt, Brian, 40–41
Simpson, Matthew, 10
Śiva, 62
Smith, Wilfred Cantwell, 6, 107, 133
Stephen of Hungary, 1

Thomas Aquinas, 78, 106
Thoreau, Henry David, 9
Tillich, Paul, 4, 47, 106, 133
Toolan, David, 126–27, 133
Trotter, F. Thomas, 8, 10

Ueda Roshii, 28
Unno, Mark, 60

Weinberg, Steven, 42
Welty, Eudora, vii, 9, 133
Wesley, John, 78
Whitehead, Alfred North, 1, 4–5, 10, 48–49, 85, 94, 100, 102, 108, 113, 115, 123–25, 128, 133

Index of Names

Williams, Daniel Day, 106
Wilson, E. O., 42
Wright, N. T., 76, 133

Yeats, William Butler, 9, 18, 43

Zhuangzi, 69

Scripture Index

Genesis
1-11   17

Psalms
23   36

Matthew
4   89
5:13   70
5:23–24   109
6:5–14   86
6:24   70
6:25   73
6:26–29   74
6:30   74
7:13–14   72
7:16   70
8:22   70
9   89–90
9:35—10:8   87
10:38   77
12:12   109
13:33   71
21:1–10   73
23:24   70
23:44   71
28   81

Mark
1:10   68
8:34   77
9:33–40   20
9:33–37   20–21
9:38-40   23
12:26–27a   123–24
14:32–42   86

Luke
6:39   70
6:44   70
9:60   70
12:24–27   74
12:28   74
13:20   71
14:16–24   73
14:26   73
14:27   77
16:13   70
19:13   73
24:5   122
24:13–35   81
24:36–49   81

John
1:1–5   12, 81, 86
1:1–3   127
1:14   127
14:27   123

Scripture Index

Acts
1 — 87

1 Corinthians
15:50–52 — 125

2 Corinthians
5:19 — 130

Philippians
2:5–9 — 39–46

Colossians
1:15–20 — 129

www.ingramcontent.com/pod-product-compliance
Lightning Source LLC
Chambersburg PA
CBHW031502160426
43195CB00010BB/1075